Singapore MATH

LEVEL 4 A&B

Thinking Kids®
An imprint of Carson Dellosa Education
Greensboro, North Carolina

P9-BZN-016

Copyright © 2015 Singapore Asia Publishers Pte. Ltd.

Thinking Kids®
An imprint of Carson Dellosa Education
PO Box 35665
Greensboro, NC 27425 USA

Printed in the USA • All rights reserved.   ISBN 978-1-4838-1321-9
08-188207784

Table of Contents

Singapore Math Level 4A & 4B

Table of Contents

Singapore Math Level 4A & 4B

INTRODUCTION TO SINGAPORE MATH

Welcome to Singapore Math! The math curriculum in Singapore has been recognized worldwide for its excellence in producing students highly skilled in mathematics. Students in Singapore have ranked at the top in the world in mathematics on the *Trends in International Mathematics and Science Study* (TIMSS) in 1993, 1995, 2003, and 2008. Because of this, Singapore Math has gained in interest and popularity in the United States.

Singapore Math curriculum aims to help students develop the necessary math concepts and process skills for everyday life and to provide students with the ability to formulate, apply, and solve problems. Mathematics in the Singapore Primary (Elementary) Curriculum cover fewer topics but in greater depth. Key math concepts are introduced and built on to reinforce various mathematical ideas and thinking. Students in Singapore are typically one grade level ahead of students in the United States.

The following pages provide examples of the various math problem types and skill sets taught in Singapore.

At an elementary level, some simple mathematical skills can help students understand mathematical principles. These skills are the counting-on, counting-back, and crossing-out methods. Note that these methods are most useful when the numbers are small.

1. The Counting-On Method

Used for addition of two numbers. Count on in 1s with the help of a picture or number line.

$$7 + 4 = \textbf{11}$$

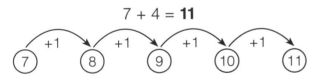

2. The Counting-Back Method

Used for subtraction of two numbers. Count back in 1s with the help of a picture or number line.

$$16 - 3 = \textbf{13}$$

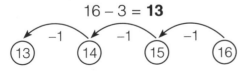

3. The Crossing-Out Method

Used for subtraction of two numbers. Cross out the number of items to be taken away. Count the remaining ones to find the answer.

$$20 - 12 = \textbf{8}$$

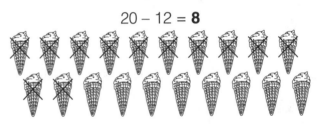

A **number bond** shows the relationship in a simple addition or subtraction problem. The number bond is based on the concept "part-part-whole." This concept is useful in teaching simple addition and subtraction to young children.

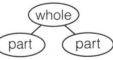

To find a whole, students must add the two parts.

To find a part, students must subtract the other part from the whole.

The different types of number bonds are illustrated on the next page.

Singapore Math Level 4A & 4B

1. Number Bond (single digits)

3 (part) + 6 (part) = **9** (whole)

9 (whole) − 3 (part) = **6** (part)

9 (whole) − 6 (part) = **3** (part)

2. Addition Number Bond (single digits)

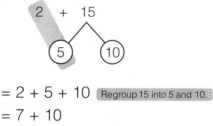

= 9 + 1 + 4   Make a ten first.

= 10 + 4

= **14**

3. Addition Number Bond (double and single digits)

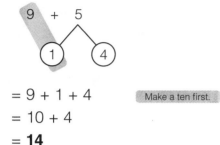

= 2 + 5 + 10   Regroup 15 into 5 and 10.

= 7 + 10

= **17**

4. Subtraction Number Bond (double and single digits)

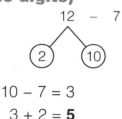

10 − 7 = 3

3 + 2 = **5**

5. Subtraction Number Bond (double digits)

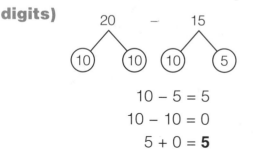

10 − 5 = 5

10 − 10 = 0

5 + 0 = **5**

Students should understand that multiplication is repeated addition and that division is the grouping of all items into equal sets.

1. Repeated Addition (Multiplication)

Mackenzie eats 2 rolls a day. How many rolls does she eat in 5 days?

$$2 + 2 + 2 + 2 + 2 = 10$$
$$5 \times 2 = 10$$

She eats **10** rolls in 5 days.

2. The Grouping Method (Division)

Mrs. Lee makes 14 sandwiches. She gives all the sandwiches equally to 7 friends. How many sandwiches does each friend receive?

$$14 \div 7 = 2$$

Each friend receives **2** sandwiches.

One of the basic but essential math skills students should acquire is to perform the 4 operations of whole numbers and fractions. Each of these methods is illustrated below.

1. The Adding-Without-Regrouping Method

H	T	O	
3	2	1	O: Ones
+ 5	6	8	T: Tens
8	**8**	**9**	H: Hundreds

Since no regrouping is required, add the digits in each place value accordingly.

2. The Adding-by-Regrouping Method

H	T	O	
¹4	9	2	O: Ones
+ 1	5	3	T: Tens
6	**4**	**5**	H: Hundreds

In this example, regroup 14 tens into 1 hundred 4 tens.

Singapore Math Level 4A & 4B

3. The Adding-by-Regrouping-Twice Method

```
  H  T  O
 ¹2 ¹8 6
+  3  6  5
───────────
   6  5  1
```

O: Ones
T: Tens
H: Hundreds

Regroup twice in this example.
First, regroup 11 ones into 1 ten 1 one.
Second, regroup 15 tens into 1 hundred 5 tens.

4. The Subtracting-Without-Regrouping Method

```
  H  T  O
  7  3  9
− 3  2  5
──────────
  4  1  4
```

O: Ones
T: Tens
H: Hundreds

Since no regrouping is required, subtract the digits in each place value accordingly.

5. The Subtracting-by-Regrouping Method

```
  H   T   O
  5  ⁷8 ¹¹1
− 2   4   7
─────────────
  3   3   4
```

O: Ones
T: Tens
H: Hundreds

In this example, students cannot subtract 7 ones from 1 one. So, regroup the tens and ones. Regroup 8 tens 1 one into 7 tens 11 ones.

6. The Subtracting-by-Regrouping-Twice Method

```
  H    T    O
 ⁷8  ⁹0  ¹⁰0
−  5   9   3
────────────────
   2   0   7
```

O: Ones
T: Tens
H: Hundreds

In this example, students cannot subtract 3 ones from 0 ones and 9 tens from 0 tens. So, regroup the hundreds, tens, and ones. Regroup 8 hundreds into 7 hundreds 9 tens 10 ones.

7. The Multiplying-Without-Regrouping Method

```
  T  O
  2  4
×     2
────────
  4  8
```

O: Ones
T: Tens

Since no regrouping is required, multiply the digit in each place value by the multiplier accordingly.

8. The Multiplying-With-Regrouping Method

```
  H  T  O
 ¹3 ²4  9
×        3
──────────
1, 0 4  7
```

O: Ones
T: Tens
H: Hundreds

In this example, regroup 27 ones into 2 tens 7 ones, and 14 tens into 1 hundred 4 tens.

9. The Dividing-Without-Regrouping Method

```
        2  4  1
    ┌──────────
  2 │ 4  8  2
    −4
    ───
       8
      −8
      ───
          2
         −2
         ───
          0
```

Since no regrouping is required, divide the digit in each place value by the divisor accordingly.

10. The Dividing-With-Regrouping Method

```
        1  6  6
    ┌──────────
  5 │ 8  3  0
    −5
    ───
      3  3
     −3  0
     ─────
         3  0
       − 3  0
       ──────
            0
```

In this example, regroup 3 hundreds into 30 tens and add 3 tens to make 33 tens. Regroup 3 tens into 30 ones.

11. The Addition-of-Fractions Method

$$\frac{1}{6} \times \frac{2}{2} + \frac{1}{4} \times \frac{3}{3} = \frac{2}{12} + \frac{3}{12} = \frac{5}{12}$$

Always remember to make the denominators common before adding the fractions.

12. The Subtraction-of-Fractions Method

$$\frac{1}{2} \times \frac{5}{5} - \frac{1}{5} \times \frac{2}{2} = \frac{5}{10} - \frac{2}{10} = \frac{3}{10}$$

Always remember to make the denominators common before subtracting the fractions.

13. The Multiplication-of-Fractions Method

$$\frac{\overset{1}{\cancel{3}}}{5} \times \frac{1}{\underset{3}{\cancel{9}}} = \frac{1}{15}$$

When the numerator and the denominator have a common multiple, reduce them to their lowest fractions.

14. The Division-of-Fractions Method

$$\frac{7}{9} \div \frac{1}{6} = \frac{7}{\underset{3}{\cancel{9}}} \times \frac{\overset{2}{\cancel{6}}}{1} = \frac{14}{3} = 4\frac{2}{3}$$

When dividing fractions, first change the division sign ($\div$) to the multiplication sign ($\times$). Then, switch the numerator and denominator of the fraction on the right hand side. Multiply the fractions in the usual way.

Model drawing is an effective strategy used to solve math word problems. It is a visual representation of the information in word problems using bar units. By drawing the models, students will know of the variables given in the problem, the variables to find, and even the methods used to solve the problem.

Drawing models is also a versatile strategy. It can be applied to simple word problems involving addition, subtraction, multiplication, and division. It can also be applied to word problems related to fractions, decimals, percentage, and ratio.

The use of models also trains students to think in an algebraic manner, which uses symbols for representation.

The different types of bar models used to solve word problems are illustrated below.

1. The model that involves addition

Melissa has 50 blue beads and 20 red beads. How many beads does she have altogether?

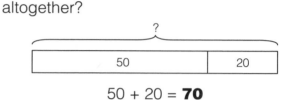

$$50 + 20 = \textbf{70}$$

2. The model that involves subtraction

Ben and Andy have 90 toy cars. Andy has 60 toy cars. How many toy cars does Ben have?

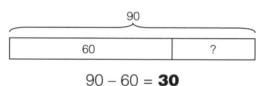

$$90 - 60 = \textbf{30}$$

3. The model that involves comparison

Mr. Simons has 150 magazines and 110 books in his study. How many more magazines than books does he have?

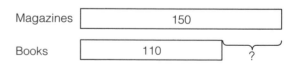

$$150 - 110 = \textbf{40}$$

4. The model that involves two items with a difference

A pair of shoes costs $109. A leather bag costs $241 more than the pair of shoes. How much is the leather bag?

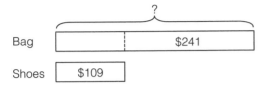

$$\$109 + \$241 = \textbf{\$350}$$

5. The model that involves multiples

Mrs. Drew buys 12 apples. She buys 3 times as many oranges as apples. She also buys 3 times as many cherries as oranges. How many pieces of fruit does she buy altogether?

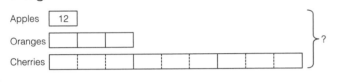

$$13 \times 12 = \textbf{156}$$

6. The model that involves multiples and difference

There are 15 students in Class A. There are 5 more students in Class B than in Class A. There are 3 times as many students in Class C than in Class A. How many students are there altogether in the three classes?

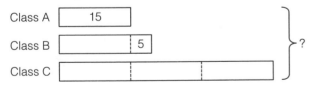

$$(5 \times 15) + 5 = \textbf{80}$$

7. The model that involves creating a whole

Ellen, Giselle, and Brenda bake 111 muffins. Giselle bakes twice as many muffins as Brenda. Ellen bakes 9 fewer muffins than Giselle. How many muffins does Ellen bake?

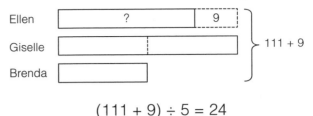

$$(111 + 9) \div 5 = 24$$
$$(2 \times 24) - 9 = \textbf{39}$$

8. The model that involves sharing

There are 183 tennis balls in Basket A and 97 tennis balls in Basket B. How many tennis balls must be transferred from Basket A to Basket B so that both baskets contain the same number of tennis balls?

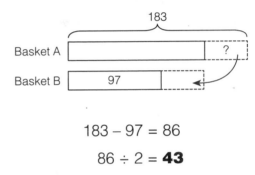

$$183 - 97 = 86$$
$$86 \div 2 = \textbf{43}$$

9. The model that involves fractions

George had 355 marbles. He lost $\frac{1}{5}$ of the marbles and gave $\frac{1}{4}$ of the remaining marbles to his brother. How many marbles did he have left?

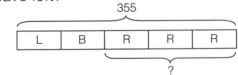

L: Lost
B: Brother
R: Remaining

$$5 \text{ parts} \rightarrow 355 \text{ marbles}$$
$$1 \text{ part} \rightarrow 355 \div 5 = 71 \text{ marbles}$$
$$3 \text{ parts} \rightarrow 3 \times 71 = \textbf{213} \text{ marbles}$$

Singapore Math Level 4A & 4B

10. The model that involves ratio

Aaron buys a tie and a belt. The prices of the tie and belt are in the ratio 2 : 5. If both items cost $539,

(a) what is the price of the tie?

(b) what is the price of the belt?

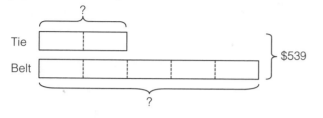

$539 ÷ 7 = $77

Tie (2 units) → 2 × $77 = **$154**

Belt (5 units) → 5 × $77 = **$385**

11. The model that involves comparison of fractions

Jack's height is $\frac{2}{3}$ of Leslie's height. Leslie's height is $\frac{3}{4}$ of Lindsay's height. If Lindsay is 160 cm tall, find Jack's height and Leslie's height.

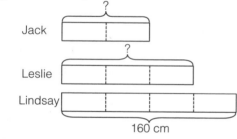

1 unit → 160 ÷ 4 = 40 cm

Leslie's height (3 units) → 3 × 40 = **120 cm**

Jack's height (2 units) → 2 × 40 = **80 cm**

Thinking skills and strategies are important in mathematical problem solving. These skills are applied when students think through the math problems to solve them. The following are some commonly used thinking skills and strategies applied in mathematical problem solving.

1. Comparing

Comparing is a form of thinking skill that students can apply to identify similarities and differences.

When comparing numbers, look carefully at each digit before deciding if a number is greater or less than the other. Students might also use a number line for comparison when there are more numbers.

Example:

3 is greater than 2 but smaller than 7.

2. Sequencing

A sequence shows the order of a series of numbers. *Sequencing* is a form of thinking skill that requires students to place numbers in a particular order. There are many terms in a sequence. The terms refer to the numbers in a sequence.

To place numbers in a correct order, students must first find a rule that generates the sequence. In a simple math sequence, students can either add or subtract to find the unknown terms in the sequence.

Example: Find the 7th term in the sequence below.

1,	4,	7,	10,	13,	16	?
1st term	2nd term	3rd term	4th term	5th term	6th term	7th term

Step 1: This sequence is in an increasing order.

Step 2: 4 − 1 = 3   7 − 4 = 3
    The difference between two consecutive terms is 3.

Step 3: 16 + 3 = 19
    The 7th term is **19**.

3. Visualization

Visualization is a problem solving strategy that can help students visualize a problem through the use of physical objects. Students will play a more active role in solving the problem by manipulating these objects.

The main advantage of using this strategy is the mobility of information in the process of solving the problem. When students make a wrong step in the process, they can retrace the step without erasing or canceling it.

The other advantage is that this strategy helps develop a better understanding of the problem or solution through visual objects or images. In this way, students will be better able to remember how to solve these types of problems.

Some of the commonly used objects for this strategy are toothpicks, straws, cards, strings, water, sand, pencils, paper, and dice.

4. Look for a Pattern

This strategy requires the use of observational and analytical skills. Students have to observe the given data to find a pattern in order to solve the problem. Math word problems that involve the use of this strategy usually have repeated numbers or patterns.

Example: Find the sum of all the numbers from 1 to 100.

Step 1: <u>Simplify the problem.</u>
Find the sum of 1, 2, 3, 4, 5, 6, 7, 8, 9, and 10.

Step 2: <u>Look for a pattern.</u>

$1 + 10 = 11 \quad 2 + 9 = 11$
$3 + 8 = 11 \quad 4 + 7 = 11$
$5 + 6 = 11$

Step 3: <u>Describe the pattern.</u>
When finding the sum of 1 to 10, add the first and last numbers to get a result of 11. Then, add the second and second last numbers to get the same result. The pattern continues until all the numbers from 1 to 10 are added. There will be 5 pairs of such results. Since each addition equals 11, the answer is then $5 \times 11 = 55$.

Step 4: <u>Use the pattern to find the answer.</u>
Since there are 5 pairs in the sum of 1 to 10, there should be ($10 \times 5 = 50$ pairs) in the sum of 1 to 100.
Note that the addition for each pair is not equal to 11 now. The addition for each pair is now ($1 + 100 = 101$).

$50 \times 101 = 5050$

The sum of all the numbers from 1 to 100 is **5,050**.

5. Working Backward

The strategy of working backward applies only to a specific type of math word problem. These word problems state the end result, and students are required to find the total number. In order to solve these word problems, students have to work backward by thinking through the correct sequence of events. The strategy of working backward allows students to use their logical reasoning and sequencing to find the answers.

Example: Sarah has a piece of ribbon. She cuts the ribbon into 4 equal parts. Each part is then cut into 3 smaller equal parts. If the length of each small part is 35 cm, how long is the piece of ribbon?

$3 \times 35 = 105$ cm
$4 \times 105 = 420$ cm

The piece of ribbon is **420 cm**.

6. The Before-After Concept

The *Before-After* concept lists all the relevant data before and after an event. Students can then compare the differences and eventually solve the problems. Usually, the Before-After concept and the mathematical model go hand in hand to solve math word problems. Note that the Before-After concept can be applied only to a certain type of math word problem, which trains students to think sequentially.

Example: Kelly has 4 times as much money as Joey. After Kelly uses some money to buy a tennis racquet, and Joey uses $30 to buy a pair of pants, Kelly has twice as much money as Joey. If Joey has $98 in the beginning,
(a) how much money does Kelly have in the end?
(b) how much money does Kelly spend on the tennis racquet?

Before

After

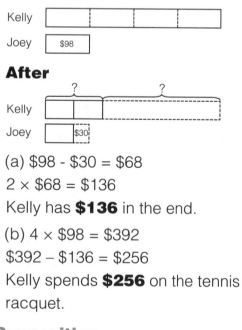

(a) $98 - $30 = $68
2 × $68 = $136
Kelly has **$136** in the end.
(b) 4 × $98 = $392
$392 – $136 = $256
Kelly spends **$256** on the tennis racquet.

7. Making Supposition

Making supposition is commonly known as "making an assumption." Students can use this strategy to solve certain types of math word problems. Making assumptions will eliminate some possibilities and simplifies the word problems by providing a boundary of values to work within.

Example: Mrs. Jackson bought 100 pieces of candy for all the students in her class. How many pieces of candy would each student receive if there were 25 students in her class?

In the above word problem, assume that each student received the same number of pieces. This eliminates the possibilities that some students would receive more than others due to good behavior, better results, or any other reason.

8. Representation of Problem

In problem solving, students often use representations in the solutions to show their understanding of the problems. Using representations also allow students to understand the mathematical concepts and relationships as well as to manipulate the information presented in the problems. Examples of representations are diagrams and lists or tables.

Diagrams allow students to consolidate or organize the information given in the problems. By drawing a diagram, students can see the problem clearly and solve it effectively.

A list or table can help students organize information that is useful for analysis. After analyzing, students can then see a pattern, which can be used to solve the problem.

12

9. Guess and Check

One of the most important and effective problem-solving techniques is *Guess and Check*. It is also known as *Trial and Error*. As the name suggests, students have to guess the answer to a problem and check if that guess is correct. If the guess is wrong, students will make another guess. This will continue until the guess is correct.

It is beneficial to keep a record of all the guesses and checks in a table. In addition, a *Comments* column can be included. This will enable students to analyze their guess (if it is too high or too low) and improve on the next guess. Be careful; this problem-solving technique can be tiresome without systematic or logical guesses.

Example: Jessica had 15 coins. Some of them were 10-cent coins and the rest were 5-cent coins. The total amount added up to $1.25. How many coins of each kind were there?

Use the guess-and-check method.

Number of 10¢ Coins	Value	Number of 5¢ Coins	Value	Total Number of Coins	Total Value
7	$7 \times 10¢ = 70¢$	8	$8 \times 5¢ = 40¢$	$7 + 8 = 15$	$70¢ + 40¢ = 110¢$ $= \$1.10$
8	$8 \times 10¢ = 80¢$	7	$7 \times 5¢ = 35¢$	$8 + 7 = 15$	$80¢ + 35¢ = 115¢$ $= \$1.15$
10	$10 \times 10¢ = 100¢$	5	$5 \times 5¢ = 25¢$	$10 + 5 = 15$	$100¢ + 25¢ = 125¢$ $= \$1.25$

There were **ten** 10-cent coins and **five** 5-cent coins.

10. Restate the Problem

When solving challenging math problems, conventional methods may not be workable. Instead, restating the problem will enable students to see some challenging problems in a different light so that they can better understand them.

The strategy of restating the problem is to "say" the problem in a different and clearer way. However, students have to ensure that the main idea of the problem is not altered.

How do students restate a math problem?

First, read and understand the problem. Gather the given facts and unknowns. Note any condition(s) that have to be satisfied.

Next, restate the problem. Imagine narrating this problem to a friend. Present the given facts, unknown(s), and condition(s). Students may want to write the "revised" problem. Once the "revised" problem is analyzed, students should be able to think of an appropriate strategy to solve it.

11. Simplify the Problem

One of the commonly used strategies in mathematical problem solving is simplification of the problem. When a problem is simplified, it can be "broken down" into two or more smaller parts. Students can then solve the parts systematically to get to the final answer.

Singapore Math Level 4A & 4B

4A LEARNING OUTCOMES

Unit 1   Whole Numbers (Part 1)
Students should be able to
- recognize and write numbers up to 100,000 in numerals and words.
- identify the correct place value.
- compare and arrange numbers up to 100,000.
- complete number patterns.

Unit 2   Whole Numbers (Part 2)
Students should be able to
- round numbers to the nearest ten or hundred.
- estimate answers involving 4 operations.
- list factors or multiples of a whole number.
- find common factors or multiples.

Review 1
This review tests students' understanding of Units 1 & 2.

Unit 3   Whole Numbers (Part 3)
Students should be able to
- multiply numbers by 1-digit and 2-digit numbers.
- divide numbers by 1-digit numbers.
- estimate answers in multiplication and division.
- check that answers are reasonable.
- solve up to 3-step story problems.

Unit 4   Line Graphs and Tables
Students should be able to
- read and understand tables and line graphs.
- complete tables using given data.
- solve problems using given data in tables and line graphs.

Review 2
This review tests students' understanding of Units 3 & 4.

Unit 5   Fractions
Students should be able to
- recognize mixed numbers and improper fractions.

- convert mixed numbers to improper fractions or improper fractions to mixed numbers.
- add and subtract fractions.
- multiply proper/improper fractions and whole numbers.
- solve up to 2-step story problems related to fractions.

Unit 6   Angles
Students should be able to
- name angles.
- measure and draw angles in degrees with the use of a protractor.
- relate a turn with degrees up to 360°.
- understand 8-point compass.

Review 3
This review tests students' understanding of Units 5 & 6.

Unit 7   Perpendicular and Parallel Lines
Students should be able to
- draw and identify perpendicular and parallel lines.
- identify vertical and horizontal lines.

Unit 8   Rectangles and Squares
Students should be able to
- recognize properties of rectangles and squares.
- find unknown lengths in rectangles and squares.
- find unknown angles in rectangles and squares.

Review 4
This review tests students' understanding of Units 7 & 8.

Final Review
This review is an excellent assessment of students' understanding of all the topics in this book.

Singapore Math Level 4A & 4B

FORMULA SHEET

Unit 1 Whole Numbers (Part 1)
5-digit numbers can be written in this manner.

Example: Write 72,948 as words.

seventy-two thousand, nine hundred, forty-eight

Place value
In a 5-digit number, each digit is in a different place and has a different value. The place value will help identify the particular place such as ten thousands, thousands, hundreds, tens, or ones and its value.

Example: In 16,258,

the digit 1 is in the **ten thousands** place.
the digit 1 stands for **10 thousands** or **10,000**.
the value of the digit 1 is **10,000**.

Comparing numbers
Start comparing the 2 numbers from the ten thousands place.
- When one number is bigger than the other, use the words *greater than* to describe it.
- When one number is smaller than the other, use the words *smaller than* to describe it.

More than and Less than
Substitute the words *more than* with an addition sign (+).

Example: What is 20,000 more than 58,324?
20,000 + 58,324 = 78,324

Similarly, substitute the words *less than* with a subtraction sign (−).

Example: What is 9,000 less than 12,685?
12,685 − 9,000 = 3,685

Order and Pattern
When arranging a set of numbers in order,
- determine if the order must begin with the largest or the smallest,
- compare the place value of the numbers,
- arrange the numbers in the correct order.

For number pattern problems,
- determine if the number pattern is in an increasing or a decreasing order,
- find the difference between 2 consecutive numbers,
- apply the difference to find the unknown number.

Unit 2 Whole Numbers (Part 2)
Rounding is to express a number to its nearest ten, hundred, or thousand.
Symbol: approximation sign (≈)
Step 1: Identify the digit to observe.
Step 2: If the digit is less than 5, round down to a lower number.
Step 3: If the digit is equal to or more than 5, round up to a higher number.
Examples: 936 ≈ 940 (when rounded off to the nearest ten)
≈ 900 (when rounded off to the nearest hundred)
Estimation gives an approximate calculation when performing addition, subtraction, multiplication, or division.

Estimation in addition/subtraction
Step 1: Round the addends/minuends/subtrahends to the nearest ten or hundred.
Step 2: Add the rounded addends/minuends/subtrahends.
Examples: 56 + 93 ≈ 60 + 90 = 150
81 − 25 ≈ 80 − 30 = 50

Estimation in multiplication
Step 1: Round the multiplicand to the nearest ten or hundred.
Step 2: Multiply the rounded multiplicand by the multiplier.
Example: $68 \times 5 \approx 70 \times 5 = 350$

Estimation in division
Step 1: Round the dividend to the nearest number for easy division.
Step 2: Divide the rounded dividend by the divisor to get the final answer.
Example: 731 ÷ 9 ≈ 720 ÷ 9 = 80

A **factor** is a number that can be divided into another number exactly.
dividend ÷ factor = quotient

A factor can also be a multiplicand or multiplier.
factor × factor = product
Example: The factors of 14 are 1, 2, 7, and 14.

A **multiple** is obtained by multiplying a number by another number.
factor × factor = multiple
Example: The multiples of 5 are 5, 10, 15, 20, 25, 30, …

Unit 3 Whole Numbers (Part 3)
Multiply 4-digit number by 1-digit number
- Multiply the digit in the ones place by the multiplier. Regroup the ones if required.
- Multiply the digit in the tens place by the multiplier. Regroup the tens if required.
- Multiply the digit in the hundreds place by the multiplier. Regroup the hundreds if required.
- Multiply the digit in the thousands place by the multiplier. Regroup the thousands if required.

Multiply 3-digit number by 2-digit number
Method 1
If the multiplier is in tens, break down the multiplier into smaller parts for easy multiplication.

Example:
$420 \times 40 = 420 \times 4 \times 10 = 1,680 \times 10 = 16,800$

Method 2
Step 1: Multiply the digit in the ones place by the digit in the ones place of the multiplier. Regroup the ones if required.
Multiply the digit in the tens place by the digit in the ones place of the multiplier. Regroup the tens if required.
Multiply the digit in the hundreds place by the digit in the ones place of the multiplier. Regroup the hundreds if required.
Step 2: Multiply the digit in the ones place by the tens of the multiplier. Regroup the ones if required.

Multiply the digit in the tens place by the tens of the multiplier. Regroup the tens if required.
Multiply the digit in the hundreds place by the tens of the multiplier. Regroup the hundreds if required.

Step 3: Add the results obtained in Steps 1 and 2 to get the final answer.

Divide 4-digit number by 1-digit number

Step 1: Divide the digit in the thousands place by the divisor. If there is a remainder, regroup the hundreds.

Step 2: Divide the hundreds by the divisor. If there is a remainder, regroup the tens.

Step 3: Divide the tens by the divisor. If there is a remainder, regroup the ones.

Step 4: Divide the ones by the divisor. Find the remainder if there is any.

Unit 4 Line Graphs and Tables

Tables

A table can consolidate data in a clear and organized manner. Use the data collected from a bar graph to complete a table. Also use the data given in the table to solve problems.

Examples:

Types of dessert	Number of customers
Apple Pie	22
Brownie	30
Chocolate Cake	10
Key Lime Pie	8

Types of dessert	Apple Pie	Brownie	Chocolate Cake	Key Lime Pie
Number of customers	22	30	10	8

Line Graphs

A line graph is another way to present data in an organized manner. Use the information given in line graphs to solve problems.

Example:

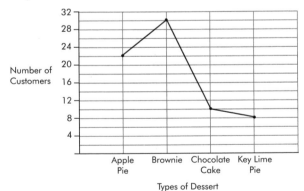

Unit 5 Fractions

A **mixed number** consists of a whole number and a fraction.

Examples: $1\frac{1}{2}$, $2\frac{1}{4}$, $5\frac{2}{5}$

An **improper fraction** is a fraction where its numerator is greater than its denominator.

Examples: $\frac{6}{5}, \frac{9}{7}, \frac{16}{7}$

Reducing fractions to their simplest form

Use the method of cancellation to reduce a fraction to its lowest term. Just divide both numerator and denominator by the same number. Ensure that such division does not have any remainder.

Example: $3\frac{4 \div 2}{6 \div 2} = 3\frac{2}{3}$

Convert a mixed number to an improper fraction

- Break the mixed number down into a whole number and a fraction.
- Convert the whole number to an improper fraction. Ensure both fractions have the same denominator.
- Add the numerator of both fractions.
- Reduce to its simplest form if needed.

Example: $6\frac{3}{8} = 6 + \frac{3}{8} = \frac{48}{8} + \frac{3}{8} = \frac{51}{8}$

Convert an improper fraction to a mixed number

Method 1

- Break the improper fraction down into the whole number in fractional form and the fraction.
- Convert the whole number in fractional form to a whole number.
- Reduce the other fraction to its simplest form if needed.
- Add the whole number and fraction.

Example: $\frac{27}{7} = \frac{21}{7} + \frac{6}{7} = 3 + \frac{6}{7} = 3\frac{6}{7}$

Method 2

- Divide the numerator by denominator.
- The quotient will be the whole number.
- The remainder will be numerator of the fraction.
- The divisor will be denominator of the fraction.

Example: $\frac{27}{7} = 27 \div 7 = 3\frac{6}{7}$

$$7\overline{)27} \quad \frac{21}{6}$$

Adding fractions

- Make sure the denominators of all fractions are common.
- Add all numerators.
- Reduce the final fraction to its simplest form.
- Convert an improper fraction to a mixed number if needed.

Example: $\frac{6}{9} + \frac{1}{3} = \frac{6}{9} + \frac{3}{9} = \frac{9}{9} = 1$

Subtracting fractions

- Make sure the denominators of all fractions are common.
- Subtract all numerators.
- Reduce the final fraction to its simplest form.
- Convert an improper fraction to a mixed number if needed.

Example: $4 - \frac{4}{7} = 3\frac{7}{7} - \frac{4}{7} = 3\frac{3}{7}$

Finding the fraction of a set

- Multiply the numerator by the whole number.
- The denominator remains the same.
- Reduce the fraction to its simplest form if needed.

Example: $\frac{4}{5}$ of $20 = \frac{4}{5} \times 20 = \frac{80}{5} = 16$

Unit 6 Angles

A **vertex** is a point whereby two lines meet to form an angle. The lines and vertex are labeled using a capital letter.

Singapore Math Level 4A & 4B

Example:

The name of the angle is ∠XYZ or ∠ZYX.
Alternatively, a small letter can represent an angle. In this example, it will be ∠a.

Measuring an angle
Use a protractor to measure an angle.

Symbol: degrees (°)

Step 1: Place the base line of a protractor on one of the lines of the angle.
Step 2: Place the center of the protractor at the vertex.
Step 3: Always read from 0°. The reading is obtained when the second line of the angle meets the marking on the protractor.

Drawing an angle
Step 1: Draw a horizontal line and mark a point centrally.
Step 2: Place the base line of a protractor on the line and the center of the protractor on the marked point.
Step 3: Measure from 0°. Mark a dot at the correct measurement. Draw a straight line through the dot to meet the horizontal line. An angle is formed.

Turns and right angles

1 right angle	$\frac{1}{4}$ of a complete turn	90°
2 right angles	$\frac{1}{2}$ of a complete turn	180°
3 right angles	$\frac{3}{4}$ of a complete turn	270°
4 right angles	1 complete turn	360°

Clockwise moves in the same direction as the movement of the clock.

Counterclockwise moves in the opposite direction as the movement of the clock.

8-point compass

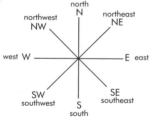

Unit 7 Perpendicular and Parallel Lines
Drawing a pair of perpendicular lines
Step 1: Use a ruler to draw a straight line. Label this line as XY.

Step 2: Place a set-square on the line and draw a vertical line. Label this line as AB.

Drawing a pair of parallel lines
Step 1: Use a ruler to draw a straight line. Label this line as AB.
Step 2: Place a set-square on the line. Next, place a ruler next to the set-square.
Step 3: Move the set-square along the ruler. Draw a line along the set-square. Label this line as CD.

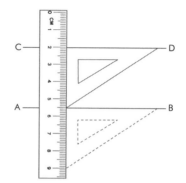

A **horizontal** line is a straight line that runs left and right, like the x-axis.
Example: _____

A **vertical** line is a line that runs up and down, like the y-axis.
Example:

Unit 8 Rectangles and Squares
Properties of a square
1. A square has four sides.
2. All four sides are equal.
3. It has two pairs of parallel lines.
4. All four angles are right angles.

Properties of a rectangle
1. A rectangle has four sides.
2. Its opposite sides are equal.
3. It has two pairs of parallel lines.
4. All four angles are right angles.

Singapore Math Level 4A & 4B

Singapore Math Level 4A & 4B

Unit 1: WHOLE NUMBERS (PART 1)

Examples:

1. What does the digit 4 stand for in 71,439?

    4 hundreds or **400**

2. What is 50,000 more than 8,395?

    $50,000 + 8,395 = $ **58,395**

3. Complete the number pattern.

    78,436, **79,486**, 80,536, 81,586

    $81,586 - 80,536 = 1,050$

    $78,436 + 1,050 = 79,486$

Write the following numbers as words on the lines.

1. 23,701 _____

2. 40,825 _____

3. 68,090 _____

4. 55,002 _____

5. 14,011 _____

Singapore Math Level 4A & 4B

Write the correct numbers in numerals on the lines.

6.   eleven thousand, six hundred, two   _____

7.   ninety-two thousand, three hundred, fourteen   _____

8.   fifty-seven thousand, twelve   _____

9.   sixty thousand, two hundred, forty-five   _____

10. eighty-two thousand, one   _____

Write the correct value of each digit in its box.

11. 15,326
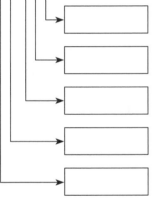

13. 78,035
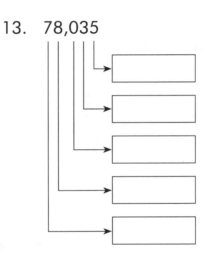

12. 58,217
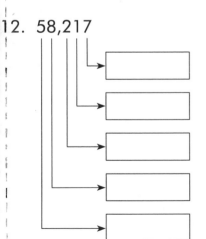

14. 81,420
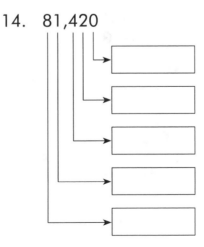

Singapore Math Level 4A & 4B

Fill in each blank with the correct answer.

15. In 64,925, the digit 6 is in the _____ place.

16. In 80,647, the digit 4 is in the _____ place.

17. In 38,416, the digit _____ is in the thousands place.

18. In 73,029, the digit _____ is in the hundreds place.

19. In 81,246,

    (a) the digit 8 stands for _____.

    (b) the digit 1 stands for _____.

    (c) the digit 2 stands for _____.

    (d) the digit 4 stands for _____.

    (e) the digit 6 stands for _____.

20. 5,217 = 5 thousands + _____ hundreds + 1 ten + 7 ones

21. 1,106 = 1 thousand + _____ hundred + 6 ones

22. 35,248 = _____ ten thousands + 5 thousands + 2 hundreds + 4 tens + 8 ones

23. 50,364 = 5 ten thousands + 3 hundreds + _____ tens + 4 ones

24. 63,724 = 60,000 + _____ + 700 + 20 + 4

25. 30,517 = 30,000 + 500 + _____ + 7

26. 10,000 + _____ + 100 = 19,100

27. 3,000 + _____ + 30 + 6 = 3,136

28. 88,627 = _____ + 8,000 + 600 + 20 + 7

Singapore Math Level 4A & 4B

29. Circle the greater number.

            48,165   49,561

30. Circle the greater number.

            98,075   97,085

31. Circle the smaller number.

            13,986   13,689

32. Circle the smaller number.

            10,738   9,173

Arrange the following numbers in ascending order.

33. 5,931,   1,359,   1,593,   5,319

_____

34. 14,632,   41,562,   24,163,   12,643

_____

35. 6,845,   4,586,   8,564,   4,685

_____

Arrange the following numbers in descending order.

36. 7,014,   1,407,   7,410,   1,740

_____

Singapore Math Level 4A & 4B

37. 39,628,   26,983,   63,892,   96,268

_____

38. 2,653,   3,652,   5,236,   5,362

_____

Complete the number patterns.

39. 226, 246, 266, _____, _____

40. 33,045, 33,050, _____, _____, 33,065

41. _____, 7,540, 7,550, _____, 7,570

42. 87,455, 88,455, 89,455, _____, _____

Fill in each blank with the correct answer.

43. _____ is 100 less than 43,112.

44. _____ is 20 less than 94,606.

45. _____ is 2,000 more than 18,096.

46. _____ is 1,000 more than 80,493.

47. 3,000 less than 21,475 is _____.

48. 100 less than 10,000 is _____.

49. 6,000 more than 4,381 is _____.

50. 99 more than 90,000 is _____.

Unit 2: WHOLE NUMBERS (PART 2)

Examples:

1. Round 798 to the nearest hundred.

$798 \approx \underline{\textbf{800}}$

2. Estimate the value of 351 − 87.

$351 - 87 \approx 350 - 90 = \underline{\textbf{260}}$

3. Estimate the value of 384 ÷ 8.

$384 \div 8 \approx 400 \div 8 = \underline{\textbf{50}}$

4. Find all the factors of 40.

$40 = 1 \times 40$
$40 = 2 \times 20$
$40 = 4 \times 10$
$40 = 5 \times 8$

The factors of 40 are $\underline{\textbf{1}}$, $\underline{\textbf{2}}$, $\underline{\textbf{4}}$, $\underline{\textbf{5}}$, $\underline{\textbf{8}}$, $\underline{\textbf{10}}$, $\underline{\textbf{20}}$, and $\underline{\textbf{40}}$.

5. Find the first five multiples of 8.

$\underline{\textbf{8}}$, $\underline{\textbf{16}}$, $\underline{\textbf{24}}$, $\underline{\textbf{32}}$, and $\underline{\textbf{40}}$

Singapore Math Level 4A & 4B

Round the following numbers to the nearest ten.

1. 771   ≈ _____

2. 848   ≈ _____

3. 661   ≈ _____

4. 296   ≈ _____

5. 1,087 ≈ _____

6. 1,782   ≈ _____

7. 39,917 ≈ _____

8. 46,547 ≈ _____

9. 11,201 ≈ _____

10. 59,999 ≈ _____

Round the following numbers to the nearest hundred.

11. 536   ≈ _____

12. 881   ≈ _____

13. 3,084 ≈ _____

14. 1,117 ≈ _____

15. 6,944 ≈ _____

16. 89,544 ≈ _____

17. 23,891 ≈ _____

18. 12,057 ≈ _____

19. 61,272 ≈ _____

20. 74,808 ≈ _____

Round the following numbers to the nearest ten and estimate their values.

21. 36 + 12 ≈ _____

22. 672 + 48 ≈ _____

23. 66 + 725 ≈ _____

24. 932 – 19 ≈ _____

25. 419 – 38 ≈ _____

26. 519 – 21 ≈ _____

Singapore Math Level 4A & 4B

Estimate the value.

27. $48 \times 8 \approx$ _____

28. $25 \times 7 \approx$ _____

29. $301 - 9 \approx$ _____

30. $697 - 88 \approx$ _____

31. $118 \div 4 \approx$ _____

32. $324 \div 5 \approx$ _____

33. $463 + 93 + 551 \approx$ _____

34. $876 + 121 + 43 \approx$ _____

Fill in each blank with the correct answer.

35. $12 =$ _____ $\times$ _____

    $12 =$ _____ $\times$ _____

    $12 =$ _____ $\times$ _____

    The factors of 12 are _____, _____, _____, _____, _____, and _____.

36. $42 =$ _____ $\times$ _____

    $42 =$ _____ $\times$ _____

    $42 =$ _____ $\times$ _____

    $42 =$ _____ $\times$ _____

    The factors of 42 are _____, _____, _____, _____, _____, _____, _____, and _____.

Singapore Math Level 4A & 4B

37. $36 = \underline{\hspace{2cm}} \times \underline{\hspace{2cm}}$

$36 = \underline{\hspace{2cm}} \times \underline{\hspace{2cm}}$

$36 = \underline{\hspace{2cm}} \times \underline{\hspace{2cm}}$

$36 = \underline{\hspace{2cm}} \times \underline{\hspace{2cm}}$

$36 = \underline{\hspace{2cm}} \times \underline{\hspace{2cm}}$

The factors of 36 are ___, ___, ___, ___, ___, ___, ___, ___, and ___.

38. (a)   The factors of 8 are _____.

(b)   The factors of 16 are _____.

(c)   The common factors of 8 and 16 are _____.

39. (a)   The factors of 14 are _____.

(b)   The factors of 28 are _____.

(c)   The common factors of 14 and 28 are _____.

40. (a)   The factors of 9 are _____.

(b)   The factors of 18 are _____.

(c)   The common factors of 9 and 18 are _____.

41.   The first four multiples of 5 are ___, ___, ___, and ___.

42.   The first three multiples of 9 are ___, ___, and ___.

43.   The third multiple of 6 is ___.

44.   The seventh multiple of 5 is ___.

45. (a)   The first six multiples of 2 are ___, ___, ___, ___, ___, and ___.

(b) The first six multiples of 3 are _____, _____, _____, _____, _____, and _____.

(c) The two common multiples of 2 and 3 are _____ and _____.

46. (a) The first six multiples of 4 are _____, _____, _____, _____, _____, and _____.

(b) The first six multiples of 8 are _____, _____, _____, _____, _____, and _____.

(c) The three common multiples of 4 and 8 are _____, _____, and _____.

Write your answers on the lines.

47. A train traveled 13,769 km from City A to City B. Then, it traveled another 25,325 km to City C. What was the estimated distance traveled by the train from City A to City C? Round each number to the nearest hundred and estimate the value.

_____

48. A number, when added to 7,982, is 25,000. Round this number to the nearest ten.

_____

49. There were 1,345 books left in a bookstore. If the shopkeeper had sold 7,609 books in the past month, how many books were in the bookstore at first? Round the answer to the nearest ten.

_____

50. In a school, there are 1,124 students in the morning session. There are 259 more students in the afternoon session than in the morning session. How many students are in the school when rounded to the nearest hundred?

_____

Singapore Math Level 4A & 4B

51. What is the smallest two-digit number that has only 4 factors?

_____

52. 8 is a factor of number X. It is between 50 and 60. What is number X?

_____

53. Number Y is a multiple of 8. It is between 20 and 30. It is also a factor of 48. What is number Y?

_____

54. If 32 is the fourth multiple of a number, what is the number?

_____

55. The two common multiples of 2 one-digit numbers are 14 and 28. If 1 is not the answer, what are the 2 one-digit numbers?

_____

REVIEW 1

Choose the correct answer. Write its number in the parentheses.

1. Which of the following shows the correct numeral for seventy-two thousand, eight hundred, forty-five?

    (1) 72,845   (3) 78,245

    (2) 72,854   (4) 78,254   (   )

2. The digit 8 in 28,095 stands for _____.

    (1) 8 ten thousands   (3) 8 hundreds

    (2) 8 thousands   (4) 8 tens   (   )

3. Which of the following is **not** a common multiple of 8 and 6?

    (1) 18   (3) 72

    (2) 24   (4) 144   (   )

4. Round each number to the nearest ten and estimate the value of 1,987 + 5,248.

    (1) 7,220   (3) 7,240

    (2) 7,230   (4) 7,250   (   )

5. Which of the following is a common factor of 28 and 36?

    (1) 3   (3) 6

    (2) 4   (4) 8   (   )

6. 9,050, _____, 7,030, 6,020, 5,010.

    What is the missing number in the pattern?

    (1) 8,020   (3) 8,040

    (2) 8,030   (4) 8,050   (   )

Singapore Math Level 4A & 4B

7. Which of the following has the greatest value?

    (1)   2,000 less than 10,000   (3)   2,000 more than 1,000

    (2)   2,000 less than 8,000   (4)   2,000 more than 800   (   )

8. Which of the following shows the first four multiples of 7?

    (1)   7, 14, 20, 27   (3)   7, 14, 28, 35

    (2)   7, 14, 21, 28   (4)   7, 14, 28, 42   (   )

9. $49,753 = $ _____ $+$ 9 thousands $+$ 7 hundreds $+$ 5 tens $+$ 3 ones

    (1)   400 ten thousands   (3)   4 ten thousands

    (2)   40 ten thousands   (4)   4 thousands   (   )

10. Estimate the value of 404×9.

    (1)   3,600   (3)   3,645

    (2)   3,636   (4)   4,000   (   )

Write your answers on the lines.

11. Write 49,005 in words.

_____

12. In 94,857, the digit 4 is in the [   ] place.   _____

13. Arrange these numbers in ascending order.

    15,050,   15,005,   15,500

_____

14. Round each number to the nearest ten and estimate its value.

    $559 + 19 + 942 \approx$ [   ]   _____

Singapore Math Level 4A & 4B

15. The seventh multiple of 9 is ☐ .   _____

16. Round 89,091 to the nearest hundred.   _____

17. 50 thousands + 90 tens + 7 ones = ☐   _____

18. List all the factors of 45.   _____

19. Add 18,360 and 2,598. The digit ☐ is in the thousands place.

                                                                 _____

20. List the first two common multiples of 4 and 6.   _____

Singapore Math Level 4A & 4B

34

Unit 3: WHOLE NUMBERS (PART 3)

Examples:

1.
$$
\begin{array}{r}
\scriptstyle 4\ 5 \\
8{,}0\ 4\ 6 \\
\times \qquad 9 \\
\hline
7\ 2{,}4\ 1\ 4 \\
\hline
\end{array}
$$

2.
$$
\begin{array}{r}
\scriptstyle 1\ 1 \\
\scriptstyle 5\ 6 \\
3\ 6\ 8 \\
\times \qquad 2\ 8 \\
\hline
2\ 9\ 4\ 4 \\
7\ 3\ 6 \\
\hline
1\ 0{,}3\ 0\ 4 \\
\hline
\end{array}
$$

3.
$$
\begin{array}{r}
1{,}5\ 5\ 7 \\
6\overline{)9{,}3\ 4\ 2} \\
6 \\
\hline
3\ 3 \\
3\ 0 \\
\hline
3\ 4 \\
3\ 0 \\
\hline
4\ 2 \\
4\ 2 \\
\hline
0 \\
\end{array}
$$

Singapore Math Level 4A & 4B

Solve the following problems. Show your work.

1.
$$\begin{array}{r} 412 \\ \times \quad 4 \\ \hline \end{array}$$

6.
$$\begin{array}{r} 5,317 \\ \times \quad 6 \\ \hline \end{array}$$

2.
$$\begin{array}{r} 547 \\ \times \quad 2 \\ \hline \end{array}$$

7.
$$\begin{array}{r} 2,011 \\ \times \quad 8 \\ \hline \end{array}$$

3.
$$\begin{array}{r} 610 \\ \times \quad 5 \\ \hline \end{array}$$

8.
$$\begin{array}{r} 6,028 \\ \times \quad 9 \\ \hline \end{array}$$

4.
$$\begin{array}{r} 935 \\ \times \quad 3 \\ \hline \end{array}$$

9.
$$\begin{array}{r} 1,526 \\ \times \quad 5 \\ \hline \end{array}$$

5.
$$\begin{array}{r} 109 \\ \times \quad 7 \\ \hline \end{array}$$

10.
$$\begin{array}{r} 8,437 \\ \times \quad 8 \\ \hline \end{array}$$

Singapore Math Level 4A & 4B

11.
$$\begin{array}{r} 46 \\ \times\ 18 \\ \hline \end{array}$$

16.
$$\begin{array}{r} 126 \\ \times\ 50 \\ \hline \end{array}$$

12.
$$\begin{array}{r} 35 \\ \times\ 20 \\ \hline \end{array}$$

17.
$$\begin{array}{r} 625 \\ \times\ 73 \\ \hline \end{array}$$

13.
$$\begin{array}{r} 67 \\ \times\ 36 \\ \hline \end{array}$$

18.
$$\begin{array}{r} 619 \\ \times\ 24 \\ \hline \end{array}$$

14.
$$\begin{array}{r} 91 \\ \times\ 27 \\ \hline \end{array}$$

19.
$$\begin{array}{r} 281 \\ \times\ 53 \\ \hline \end{array}$$

15.
$$\begin{array}{r} 89 \\ \times\ 16 \\ \hline \end{array}$$

20.
$$\begin{array}{r} 380 \\ \times\ 36 \\ \hline \end{array}$$

Singapore Math Level 4A & 4B

Solve the following problems. Show your work.

21. $5 \overline{)1,355}$

24. $8 \overline{)6,088}$

22. $3 \overline{)4,827}$

25. $6 \overline{)1,458}$

23. $2 \overline{)9,804}$

26. $3 \overline{)1,131}$

Fill in each blank with the correct answer.

27. $18 \times 20 = \underline{\hspace{1cm}} \times \underline{\hspace{1cm}}$ tens

    $= \underline{\hspace{1cm}}$ tens

    $= \underline{\hspace{1cm}}$

28. $69 \times 40 = \underline{\hspace{1cm}} \times \underline{\hspace{1cm}}$ tens

    $= \underline{\hspace{1cm}}$ tens

    $= \underline{\hspace{1cm}}$

Singapore Math Level 4A & 4B

29. 98 × 30 = _____ × _____ tens

= _____ tens

= _____

30. 53 × 60 = _____ × _____ × 10

= _____ × 10

= _____

31. 77 × 90 = _____ × _____ × 10

= _____ × 10

= _____

32. 42 × 80 = _____ × _____ × 10

= _____ × 10

= _____

33. 4,569 ÷ 8 = _____ R _____

34. 1,348 ÷ 5 = _____ R _____

35. 4,240 ÷ 7 = _____ R _____

36. 3,134 ÷ 4 = _____ R _____

37. 9,381 ÷ 9 = _____ R _____

38. 59 × 17 ≈ _____ × _____

= _____

Singapore Math Level 4A & 4B

39. $623 \times 55 \approx$ _____ $\times$ _____

$=$ _____

40. $917 \times 31 \approx$ _____ $\times$ _____

$=$ _____

41. $237 \div 5 \approx$ _____ $\div 5$

$=$ _____

42. $4{,}927 \div 7 \approx$ _____ $\div 7$

$=$ _____

43. $8{,}080 \div 9 \approx$ _____ $\div 9$

$=$ _____

44. (a) Multiply 84 by 52. _____

(b) Estimate the value of 84×52. _____

(c) State if your actual answer is reasonable. _____

45. (a) Multiply 409 by 93. _____

(b) Estimate the value of 409×93. _____

(c) State if your actual answer is reasonable. _____

46. (a) Multiply 976 by 38. _____

(b) Estimate the value of 976×38. _____

(c) State if your actual answer is reasonable. _____

Singapore Math Level 4A & 4B

47. (a) Divide 43 by 8. _____

   (b) Estimate the value of 43 ÷ 8. _____

   (c) State if your actual answer is reasonable. _____

48. (a) Divide 538 by 6. _____

   (b) Estimate the value of 538 ÷ 6. _____

   (c) State if your actual answer is reasonable. _____

49. (a) Divide 8,765 by 4. _____

   (b) Estimate the value of 8,765 ÷ 4. _____

   (c) State if your actual answer is reasonable. _____

Solve the following story problems. Show your work in the space below.

50. There are 255 balloons in a package. How many balloons are there in a dozen packages?

Singapore Math Level 4A & 4B

51. A factory makes 2,275 watches in a week. How many watches does it make in 3 days?

52. A shirt costs $253 and a tie costs $78. David bought 4 shirts and 3 ties. How much did he spend altogether?

53. A purse costs 4 times as much as a dress. If the purse costs $276, how much does Anna spend on the purse and 3 dresses?

Singapore Math Level 4A & 4B

54. Jason had some marbles. He gave 35 marbles to each of his 4 brothers and still had 219 marbles left. How many marbles did Jason have to begin with?

55. 114 men and 686 women went to a concert. Each ticket cost $17. How much money was collected in all?

56. A baker bakes 840 loaves of bread in a day. How many loaves of bread will he bake in 6 weeks?

57. Cecilia has 896 stickers. She gives 50 stickers to seven of her friends. She sorts the remaining stickers equally into three albums. How many stickers are there in each album?

58. There were 400 pieces of candy in a package. The principal of a school bought 25 packages for 2,000 children on Halloween.

   (a)   How many pieces of candy did the principal buy altogether?

   (b)   If each child was given 7 pieces, how many more packages were needed?

59. Kimi is 16 years old and her mother is 44 years old this year. How many years ago was Kimi's mother five times as old as Kimi?

60. A stereo costs $328. A television set costs four times as much as the stereo. Mr. Simon buys the stereo and the television set and pays for them in eight monthly installments. How much must he pay for them each month?

61. Michael had $3,600. After spending $320, he still had twice as much as Cynthia. Find the total amount of money they had in the beginning.

Singapore Math Level 4A & 4B

62. Luis bought a book and four identical pens for $12. Carlos bought the same book and two similar pens. Carlos paid $4 less than Luis. What was the cost of the book?

63. 250 adults and some children went to the zoo. The admission ticket for each adult was $12 and the admission ticket for each child was $9. If $6,915 was collected for all the tickets, how many children went to the zoo?

64. Mr. Ortiz received a bonus. He gave $2,000 to his wife and distributed an amount of money equally among his six children. He was left with $1,350, which was $400 more than the amount of money he gave to each child. How much was his bonus?

Singapore Math Level 4A & 4B

Unit 4: LINE GRAPHS AND TABLES

Example:

The line graph shows the number of gold, silver, and bronze medals given out during an international sports meet.

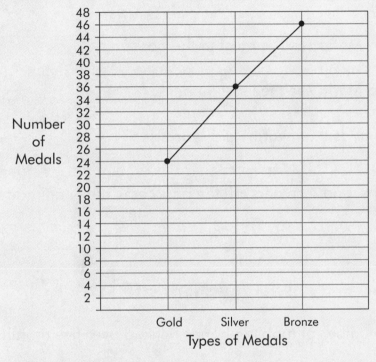

1. How many gold medals were given out?

   24

2. How many silver and bronze medals were given out?

   36 + 46 = **82** silver and bronze medals

3. How many more bronze than gold medals were given out?

   46 − 24 = **22** more bronze medals

4. If there were 58 participants who did not receive any medals, how many participants were there altogether?

   24 + 36 + 46 + 58 = **164** participants

Singapore Math Level 4A & 4B

Study the table below and answer questions 1 to 5.

The table shows the number of animals Mario saw in a park.

Animals	Spider	Bird	Cat	Worm
Number of animals	8	?	3	8

1. If there were 30 animals in the park, how many birds were there?

   _____

2. Which animal did Mario see the most in the park?   _____

3. Which animal did Mario see the least in the park?   _____

4. How many more birds than worms did Mario see?   _____

5. If 3 birds, 5 worms, and 4 spiders left the park, how many animals remained in the park?

   _____

Study the data below and answer questions 6 to 11.

Mr. Cox recorded the number of mobile phones he sold over five months in the table below.

November	JHT JHT JHT JHT JHT JHT JHT JHT JHT JHT JHT JHT JHT
December	JHT JHT JHT JHT JHT JHT
January	JHT JHT JHT JHT JHT JHT JHT JHT JHT JHT JHT JHT JHT JHT
February	JHT JHT JHT JHT JHT JHT JHT JHT JHT JHT
March	JHT JHT JHT JHT JHT JHT JHT JHT

6. Use numbers to complete the table using the data.

Months	Number of mobile phones sold
November	
December	
January	
February	
March	

7. In which month did Mr. Cox sell the most number of mobile phones?

_____

8. How many more mobile phones did Mr. Cox sell in February than in December?

_____

9. How many mobile phones were sold altogether in the two months with the highest sales?

_____

10. If the number of mobile phones sold in April was twice as many as those sold in March, how many mobile phones were sold in April?

_____

11. If each mobile phone was sold for $102, how much money did Mr. Cox make in February and March?

_____

Singapore Math Level 4A & 4B

Study the line graph and answer questions 12 to 16.

The line graph shows the number of students taking the school bus over a few years.

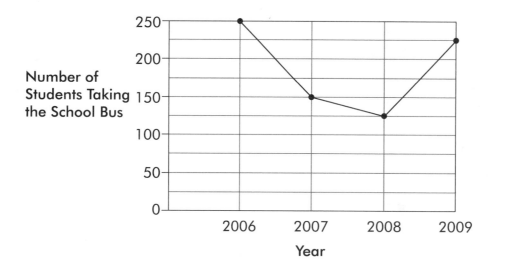

12. How many students took the school bus in 2007? _____

13. In which year was the number of students taking the school bus the greatest?

_____

14. What was the increase in the number of students taking the school bus from 2008 to 2009?

_____

15. What was the difference between the year with the greatest number of students taking the school bus and the year with the lowest number of students taking the school bus?

_____

16. How many students took the school bus from 2006 to 2009?

_____

Singapore Math Level 4A & 4B

Study the bar graph and answer questions 17 to 22.

The bar graph shows the amount of money collected by six children in a donation drive.

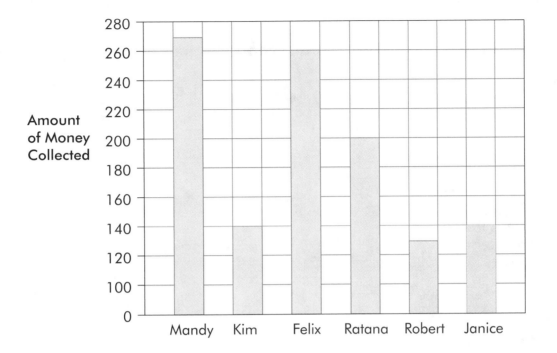

17. Using the data from the bar graph, complete the table below.

Name	Amount of money collected
Mandy	
Kim	
Felix	
Ratana	
Robert	
Janice	

18. Who collected more than $200? _____

19. Which two children collected the same amount of money? _____

20. Who collected twice as much money as Robert? _____

21. How much money was collected altogether? _____

Singapore Math Level 4A & 4B

22. How much more money did the children have to collect in order to reach $2,000?

_____

Study the line graph below and answer questions 23 to 27.

The line graph shows the number of visitors to the science center in a month.

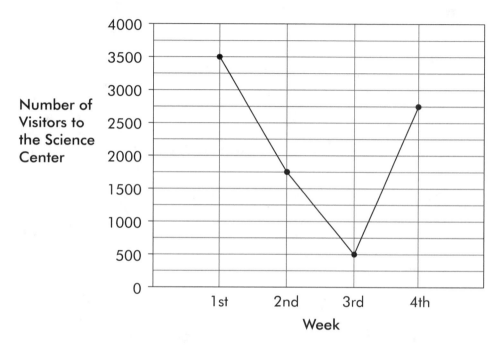

23. In which week was the number of visitors the least?   _____

24. What was the increase in the number of visitors from the 3rd to the 4th week?

_____

25. What was the decrease in the number of visitors from the 1st to the 2nd week?

_____

26. What was the difference in the week with the greatest number of visitors and the week with the lowest number of visitors?

_____

27. If each admission ticket cost $9, how much did the science center collect during the four weeks?

_____

Singapore Math Level 4A & 4B

REVIEW 2

Choose the correct answer. Write its number in the parentheses.

1. The product of 943 and 57 is _____.

    (1) 886   (3) 53,175

    (2) 1,000   (4) 53,751   (   )

2. The quotient of 7,256 ÷ 10 is _____.

    (1) 6   (3) 72

    (2) 56   (4) 725   (   )

The table shows the heights of four boys. Study the table below and answer questions 3 and 4.

Name	Height
Hakeem	140 cm
Salim	?
Colin	142 cm
Derrick	136 cm

3. If the total height of the four boys is 557 cm, what is Salim's height?

    (1) 138 cm   (3) 140 cm

    (2) 139 cm   (4) 141 cm   (   )

4. What is the difference between Salim's height and Derrick's height?

    (1) 2 cm   (3) 4 cm

    (2) 3 cm   (4) 6 cm   (   )

The line graph shows Felicia's test scores in mathematics from February to May. Study the line graph and answer questions 5 to 7.

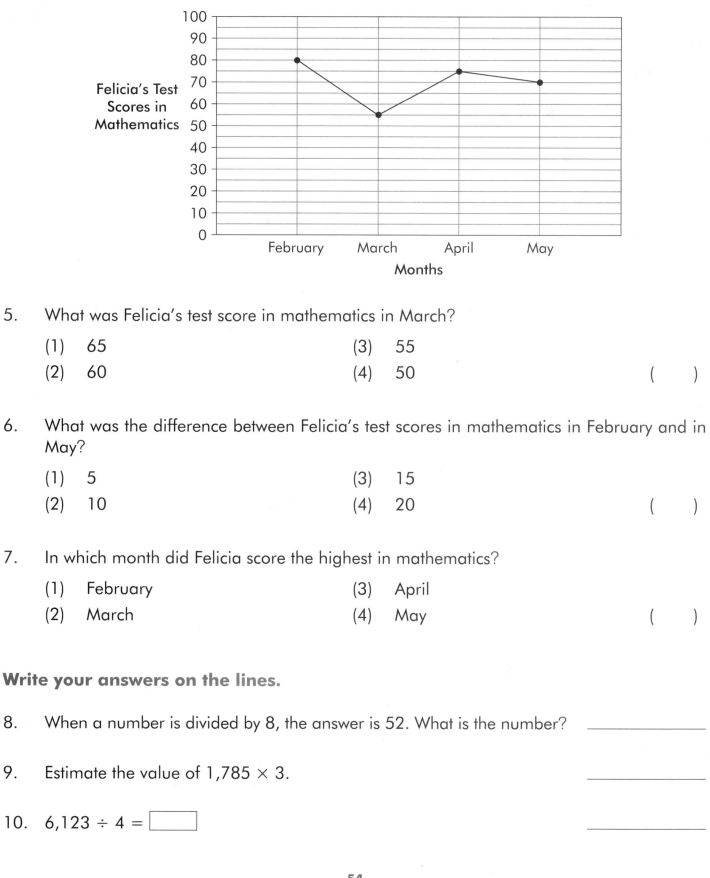

5.   What was Felicia's test score in mathematics in March?

(1)   65   (3)   55

(2)   60   (4)   50   (   )

6.   What was the difference between Felicia's test scores in mathematics in February and in May?

(1)   5   (3)   15

(2)   10   (4)   20   (   )

7.   In which month did Felicia score the highest in mathematics?

(1)   February   (3)   April

(2)   March   (4)   May   (   )

Write your answers on the lines.

8.   When a number is divided by 8, the answer is 52. What is the number?   _____

9.   Estimate the value of 1,785 × 3.   _____

10.   6,123 ÷ 4 = ☐   _____

The table shows the number of stamps and coins Dora collected from four different countries. Study the table below and answer questions 11 to 13.

Country	Stamps	Coins
Malaysia	394	127
Indonesia	?	245
Thailand	125	169
Philippines	178	88

11. If Dora collected a total of 947 stamps, how many Indonesian stamps did she collect?

_____

12. What was the total number of coins collected by Dora?   _____

13. How many more stamps than coins did Dora collect?   _____

14.   2 0 5
     ×   8 3
     _____

15. 8)7,9 1 6

Solve the following story problems. Show your work in the space below.

16. Mrs. Kim bought two boxes of pens. Both boxes contained a total of 900 pens. The bigger box contained 120 more pens than the other one. How many pens were in the smaller box?

17. Mr. Santiago bought 36 bicycles, each at $159. He sold all of them for $8,000. How much money did he earn?

18. Tai has 1,230 beads. He has three times as many beads as Reta. Veronica has half as many beads as Reta. How many beads do the three children have altogether?

Singapore Math Level 4A & 4B

19. A publisher printed 3,000 books. 54 books were found to be defective and thrown away, and the rest were sold at $9 each. How much money did the publisher make from the sale of the books?

20. A factory makes 1,395 remote-controlled cars in a week.

   (a) How many remote-controlled cars can the factory make in eight weeks?

   (b) If the factory needs to make 40,455 remote-controlled cars in nine weeks, how many remote-controlled cars must the factory make in a week?

Singapore Math Level 4A & 4B

Unit 5: FRACTIONS

Examples:

1. Convert $\frac{16}{7}$ into a mixed number.

   $$\frac{16}{7} = \frac{14}{7} + \frac{2}{7} = 2 + \frac{2}{7} = \mathbf{2\frac{2}{7}}$$

2. Convert $4\frac{5}{9}$ into an improper fraction.

   $$4\frac{5}{9} = \frac{36}{9} + \frac{5}{9} = \frac{\mathbf{41}}{\mathbf{9}}$$

3. What is the sum of $\frac{2}{3}$ and $\frac{8}{9}$? Write your answer in its simplest form.

   $$\frac{2^{\times 3}}{3^{\times 3}} + \frac{8}{9} = \frac{6}{9} + \frac{8}{9} = \frac{14}{9} = \mathbf{1\frac{5}{9}}$$

4. Find the value of $\frac{1}{3}$ of 72.

   $$\frac{1}{\cancel{3}_1} \times \cancel{72}^{24} = \mathbf{24}$$

Write the correct mixed number on the lines.

1. $3 + \frac{1}{2} = $ _____

2. $6 + \frac{2}{3} = $ _____

3. $5 + \frac{1}{4} = $ _____

4. $9 + \frac{1}{12} = $ _____

5. $7 + \dfrac{5}{7} =$ _____

8. $\dfrac{3}{5} + 2 =$ _____

6. $\dfrac{5}{8} + 4 =$ _____

9. $\dfrac{1}{6} + 8 =$ _____

7. $\dfrac{4}{9} + 1 =$ _____

10. $\dfrac{9}{11} + 3 =$ _____

Fill in each blank with the correct answer.

11.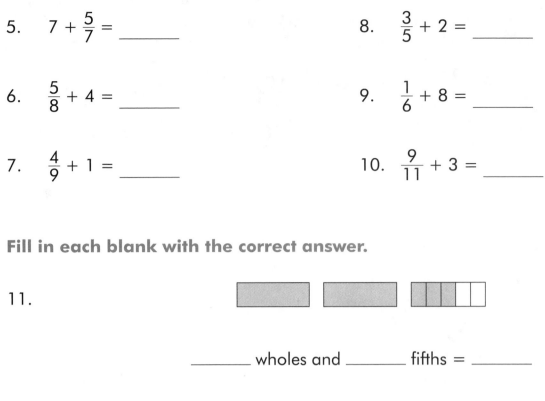

_____ wholes and _____ fifths = _____

12.

_____ wholes and _____ sevenths = _____

13.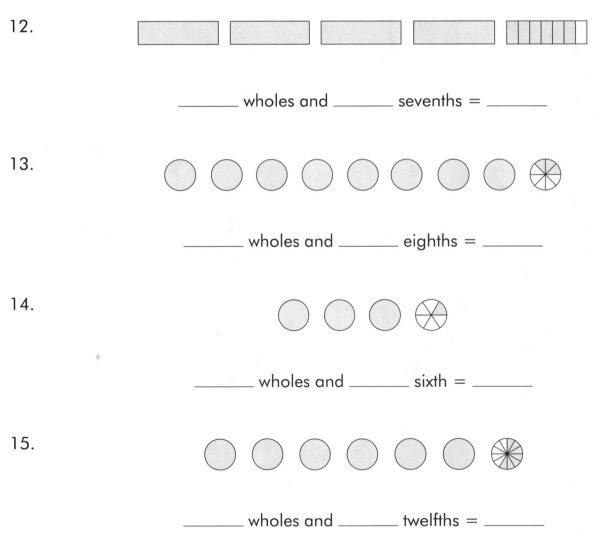

_____ wholes and _____ eighths = _____

14.

_____ wholes and _____ sixth = _____

15.

_____ wholes and _____ twelfths = _____

Singapore Math Level 4A & 4B

For each number line, write the correct mixed number in each box.

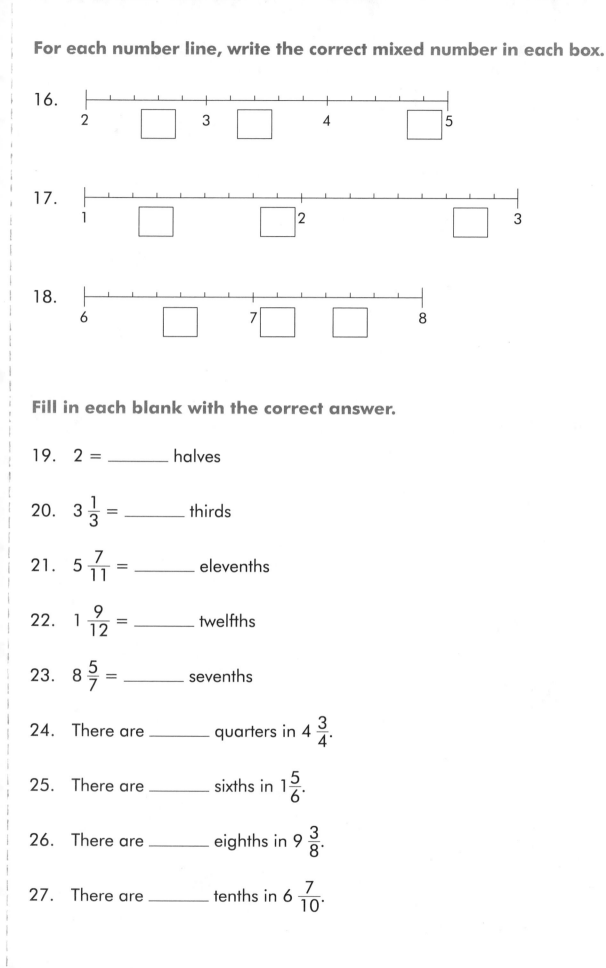

16. 2 □ 3 □ 4 □ 5

17. 1 □ □ 2 □ 3

18. 6 □ 7 □ □ 8

Fill in each blank with the correct answer.

19. $2 = $ _____ halves

20. $3\frac{1}{3} = $ _____ thirds

21. $5\frac{7}{11} = $ _____ elevenths

22. $1\frac{9}{12} = $ _____ twelfths

23. $8\frac{5}{7} = $ _____ sevenths

24. There are _____ quarters in $4\frac{3}{4}$.

25. There are _____ sixths in $1\frac{5}{6}$.

26. There are _____ eighths in $9\frac{3}{8}$.

27. There are _____ tenths in $6\frac{7}{10}$.

Singapore Math Level 4A & 4B

For each number line, write the correct improper fraction in each box. Write each improper fraction in its simplest form.

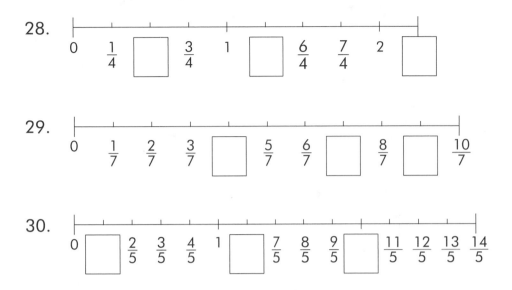

28.

| 0 | $\frac{1}{4}$ | ☐ | $\frac{3}{4}$ | 1 | ☐ | $\frac{6}{4}$ | $\frac{7}{4}$ | 2 | ☐ |

29.

| 0 | $\frac{1}{7}$ | $\frac{2}{7}$ | $\frac{3}{7}$ | ☐ | $\frac{5}{7}$ | $\frac{6}{7}$ | ☐ | $\frac{8}{7}$ | ☐ | $\frac{10}{7}$ |

30.

| 0 | ☐ | $\frac{2}{5}$ | $\frac{3}{5}$ | $\frac{4}{5}$ | 1 | ☐ | $\frac{7}{5}$ | $\frac{8}{5}$ | $\frac{9}{5}$ | ☐ | $\frac{11}{5}$ | $\frac{12}{5}$ | $\frac{13}{5}$ | $\frac{14}{5}$ |

Write each mixed number as an improper fraction.

31. $1\frac{1}{2} =$

32. $1\frac{3}{10} =$

33. $2\frac{3}{4} =$

34. $4\frac{3}{5} =$

35. $7\frac{1}{6} =$

36. $8\frac{2}{3} =$

37. $3\frac{5}{8} =$

38. $3\frac{7}{12} =$

39. $8\frac{4}{9} =$

40. $2\frac{4}{7} =$

Write each improper fraction as a mixed number.

41. $\frac{11}{2} =$

42. $\frac{9}{4} =$

43. $\frac{5}{5} =$

44. $\frac{16}{2} =$

Singapore Math Level 4A & 4B

45. $\dfrac{37}{5} =$

46. $\dfrac{12}{3} =$

47. $\dfrac{15}{8} =$

48. $\dfrac{17}{6} =$

49. $\dfrac{23}{6} =$

50. $\dfrac{38}{9} =$

Add these fractions. Write each answer in its simplest form.

51. $\dfrac{2}{5} + \dfrac{4}{5} =$

52. $\dfrac{2}{3} + \dfrac{4}{9} =$

53. $\dfrac{3}{7} + \dfrac{13}{14} =$

54. $\dfrac{5}{8} + \dfrac{3}{4} =$

55. $\dfrac{7}{12} + \dfrac{2}{6} + \dfrac{9}{12} =$

56. $\dfrac{1}{2} + \dfrac{3}{10} + \dfrac{9}{10} =$

57. $\dfrac{2}{4} + \dfrac{7}{8} + \dfrac{1}{4} =$

58. $\dfrac{1}{3} + \dfrac{3}{9} + \dfrac{5}{9} =$

Subtract these fractions. Write each answer in its simplest form.

59. $6 - \dfrac{2}{8} =$

60. $10 - \dfrac{5}{12} =$

61. $\dfrac{8}{9} - \dfrac{2}{9} =$

62. $\dfrac{9}{10} - \dfrac{1}{2} =$

63. $2\dfrac{6}{9} - \dfrac{1}{3} =$

64. $4\dfrac{9}{12} - \dfrac{2}{4} =$

65. $5\dfrac{7}{12} - \dfrac{1}{4} =$

66. $7 - \dfrac{9}{10} - \dfrac{2}{5} =$

Solve the problems below.

67. $\frac{2}{3}$ of 21 =

68. $\frac{1}{8}$ of 72 =

69. $\frac{5}{9}$ of 81 =

70. $\frac{4}{5}$ of 65 =

71. $\frac{9}{10}$ of 20 =

72. $\frac{5}{6} \times 48 =$

73. $\frac{3}{7} \times 63 =$

74. $\frac{3}{4} \times 52 =$

75. $\frac{4}{9} \times 27 =$

76. $\frac{1}{6} \times 84 =$

Solve the following story problems. Show your work in the space below.

77. Judi baked a cake. She gave $\frac{3}{8}$ of it to her neighbor. What fraction of the cake did she have left?

78. An empty can has a mass of $\frac{1}{6}$ lb. When it is filled with sand, it has a mass of $\frac{7}{12}$ lb. Find the mass of the sand in the can.

Singapore Math Level 4A & 4B

79. What is the total mass of three boxes if Box A has a mass of $\frac{5}{6}$ kg, Box B has a mass of $\frac{1}{10}$ kg, and Box C has a mass of $\frac{9}{10}$ kg?

80. After cutting a length of ribbon and giving $\frac{5}{12}$ m of ribbon to her daughter, Mrs. Kwan had $\frac{1}{4}$ m of ribbon left. If she had $\frac{11}{12}$ m of ribbon in the beginning, what was the length of ribbon Mrs. Kwan cut?

81. Maggie, Joyce, and Lina each prepared different amounts of fruit punch for a party. Maggie prepared $\frac{5}{9}$ L of fruit punch and Joyce prepared $\frac{1}{3}$ L of fruit punch. If they had prepared a total of $1\frac{2}{3}$ L of fruit punch, how much fruit punch did Lina prepare?

Singapore Math Level 4A & 4B

82. Eduardo drank $\frac{6}{10}$ L of milk. Viktor drank $\frac{1}{2}$ L of milk less than Eduardo. How much milk did the two children drink in all?

83. Mrs. Nguyen bought 5 L of cooking oil. She used $\frac{1}{4}$ L of cooking oil on Monday. She used $\frac{1}{8}$ L of cooking oil on Tuesday. How much cooking oil did she have left?

84. In a race, Carla ran $\frac{3}{4}$ km and swam $\frac{3}{8}$ km. She biked the rest of the race. If she traveled $12\frac{7}{8}$ km altogether, how far did she bike?

85. There are 16 red beads, 24 green beads, and 20 blue beads in a box. What fraction of the beads in the box are blue?

86. The distance from Town A to Town B is 18 miles. Luke starts his journey from Town A and travels $\frac{1}{6}$ of the total distance. How much further does he have to travel in order to reach Town B?

87. There were 32 chocolates in a box. After eating some chocolates, Tara found that she had $\frac{5}{8}$ of the chocolates left. How many chocolates did Tara eat?

Singapore Math Level 4A & 4B

88. Farmer Bill had 28 chickens, 15 ducks, and 7 turkeys. He sold $\frac{4}{5}$ of the birds.

   (a)   How many birds did he sell in all?

   (b)   If he sold 12 chickens, what fraction of the chickens were left?

89. 568 people watched a concert. $\frac{5}{8}$ of the audience were women, while $\frac{1}{4}$ of them were men. How many children were there at the concert?

90. Isabel received a sum of money. She gave $\frac{1}{3}$ of the money to her brother. If she had $60 left, how much money did Isabel receive?

Unit 6: ANGLES

Examples:

1. Draw an angle equal to 135°.

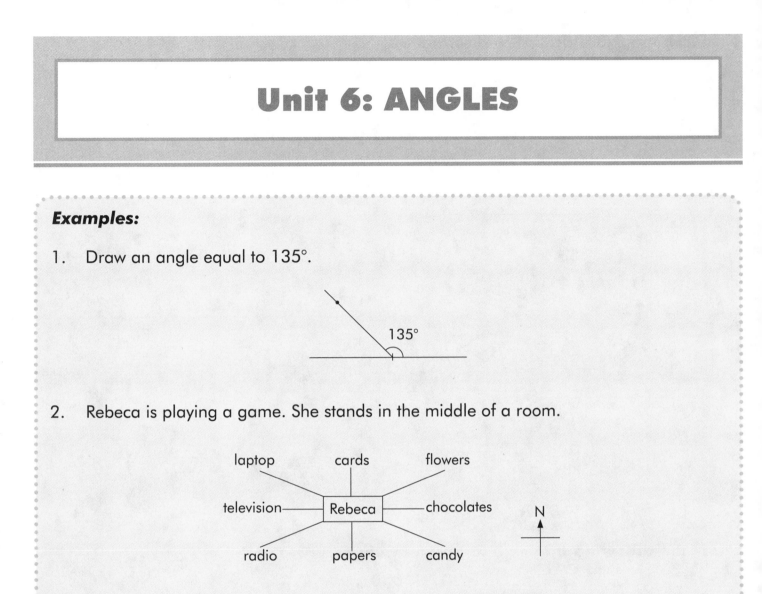

2. Rebeca is playing a game. She stands in the middle of a room.

    (a) Rebeca is facing northwest. What can she see?

    <u>laptop</u>

    (b) Rebeca is facing south. If she turns 90° counterclockwise, what will she see?

    <u>chocolates</u>

    (c) Rebeca will see the flowers if she turns 180° clockwise. In which direction is Rebeca facing?

    <u>southwest</u>

    (d) Rebeca is looking at the papers. If she turns **<u>315°</u>** counterclockwise, she will see the radio.

Singapore Math Level 4A & 4B

Name the marked angles in another way.

1.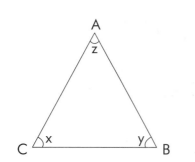

$\angle ABC =$ _____

$\angle ACB =$ _____

$\angle BAC =$ _____

2.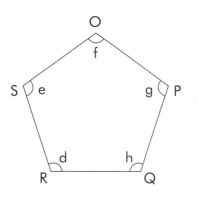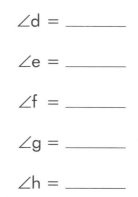

$\angle d =$ _____

$\angle e =$ _____

$\angle f =$ _____

$\angle g =$ _____

$\angle h =$ _____

Study the following angles and answer questions 3 and 4.

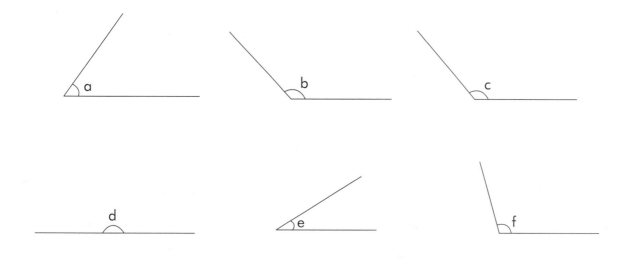

3. Identify the angles that are greater than 90°.   _____

4. Identify the angles that are smaller than 90°.   _____

Singapore Math Level 4A & 4B

Estimate and measure the marked angles with a protractor.

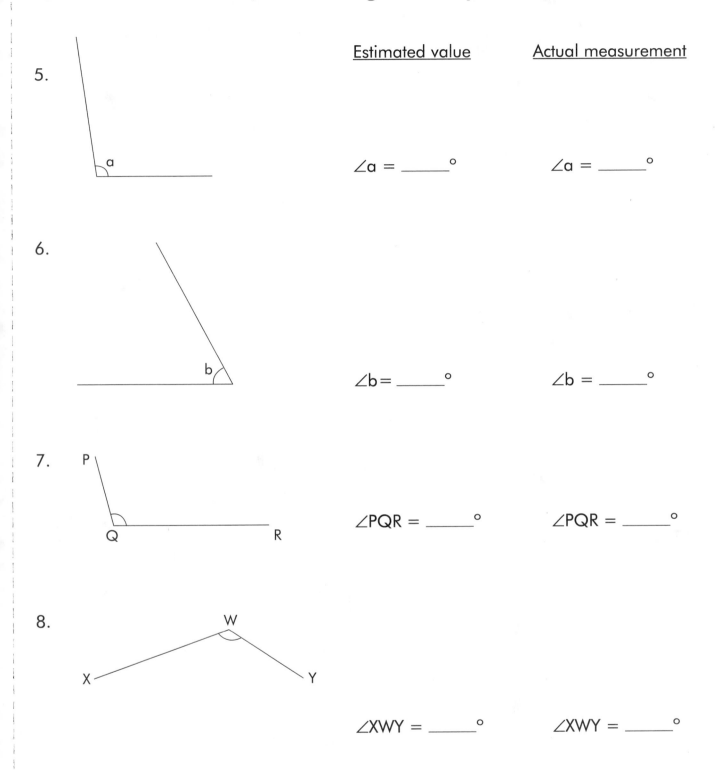

	Estimated value	Actual measurement
5.	∠a = _____°	∠a = _____°
6.	∠b = _____°	∠b = _____°
7.	∠PQR = _____°	∠PQR = _____°
8.	∠XWY = _____°	∠XWY = _____°

71

Draw the following angles in the space below.

9. $\angle p = 75°$

10. $\angle r = 108°$

11. $\angle q = 45°$

12. $\angle s = 134°$

Fill in each blank with the correct answer.

13. A _____-turn equals 1 right angle.

14. A half-turn equals _____°.

15. A _____-turn equals 270°.

16. A complete turn equals _____ right angles.

17. _____ of a complete turn is 180°.

18. _____ of a complete turn is 90°.

19. Which direction is each child from X?

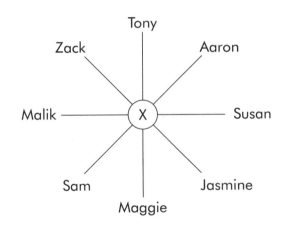

Tony: _____

Aaron: _____

Susan: _____

Jasmine: _____

Maggie: _____

Sam: _____

Malik: _____

Zack: _____

Look at each picture carefully and fill in each blank with the correct answer.

20.

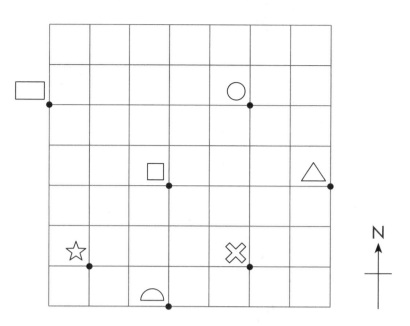

(a)   The circle is _____ of the triangle.

(b)   The semicircle is _____ of the star.

(c)   The square is _____ of the triangle.

(d)   The cross is _____ of the star.

(e)   The square is _____ of the semicircle.

(f)   The circle is _____ of the rectangle.

(g)   The triangle is _____ of the cross.

(h)   The star is _____ of the circle.

Singapore Math Level 4A & 4B

21.

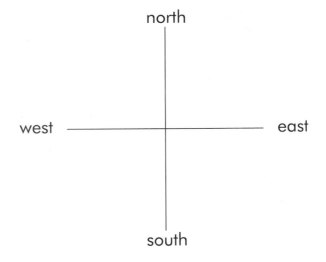

(a)   George is facing north. If he turns clockwise _____°, he will face southwest.

(b)   George is facing west. If he turns counterclockwise _____°, he will face east.

(c)   George is facing northwest. If he turns counterclockwise _____°, he will face northeast.

(d)   George is facing south. If he turns counterclockwise _____° , he will face southeast.

(e)   George is facing east. If he makes a _____-turn clockwise, he will face south.

(f)   George is facing north. If he makes a _____-turn counterclockwise, he will face east.

Singapore Math Level 4A & 4B

REVIEW 3

Choose the correct answer. Write its number in the parentheses.

1. Express $6\frac{7}{9}$ as an improper fraction.

   (1) $\frac{22}{9}$ (3) $\frac{61}{9}$

   (2) $\frac{54}{9}$ (4) $\frac{67}{9}$ (   )

2. What is the difference between $\frac{2}{5}$ and $\frac{3}{10}$?

   (1) $\frac{3}{5}$ (3) $\frac{1}{5}$

   (2) $\frac{1}{2}$ (4) $\frac{1}{10}$ (   )

3. $\frac{4}{9} + \frac{2}{3} = $ _____

   (1) $\frac{2}{3}$ (3) $\frac{6}{9}$

   (2) $\frac{2}{9}$ (4) $1\frac{1}{9}$ (   )

4. What fraction of the figure below is shaded?

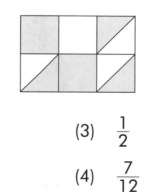

   (1) $\frac{1}{3}$ (3) $\frac{1}{2}$

   (2) $\frac{5}{12}$ (4) $\frac{7}{12}$ (   )

Singapore Math Level 4A & 4B

5. $\frac{2}{7}$ of 98 = _____

   (1)   28   (3)   196
   (2)   49   (4)   343   (   )

6. How many sixths are there in $5\frac{1}{6}$?

   (1)   3   (3)   31
   (2)   12   (4)   57   (   )

7. Measure ∠a.

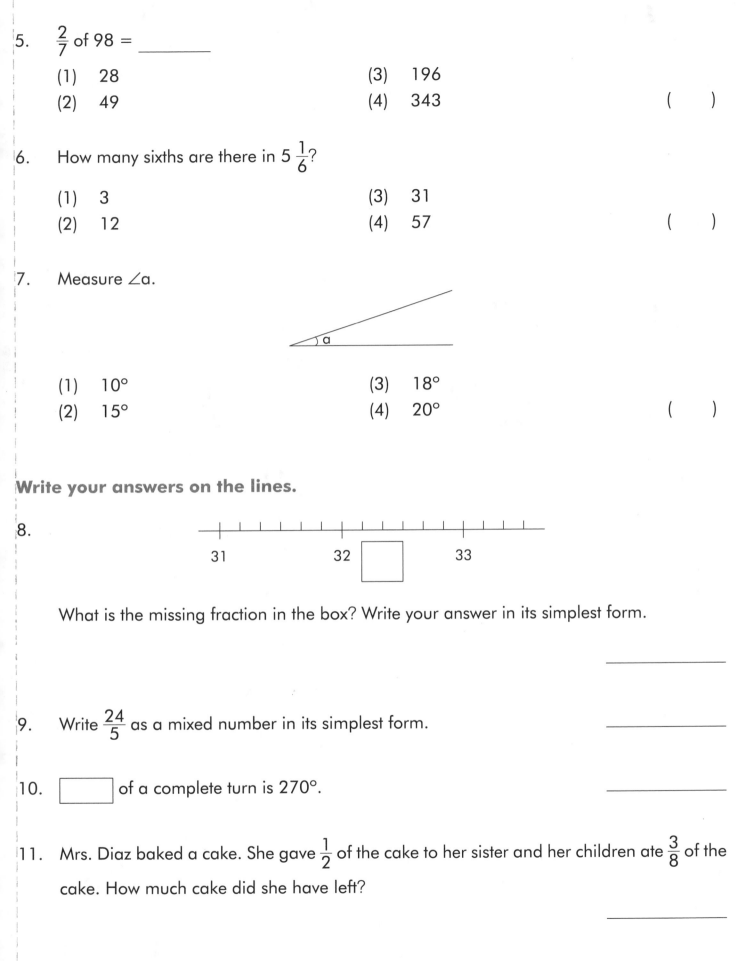

   (1)   10°   (3)   18°
   (2)   15°   (4)   20°   (   )

Write your answers on the lines.

8.

   31   32   □   33

   What is the missing fraction in the box? Write your answer in its simplest form.

   _____

9. Write $\frac{24}{5}$ as a mixed number in its simplest form.   _____

10. ☐ of a complete turn is 270°.   _____

11. Mrs. Diaz baked a cake. She gave $\frac{1}{2}$ of the cake to her sister and her children ate $\frac{3}{8}$ of the cake. How much cake did she have left?

   _____

12. Name the angle marked a in another way.

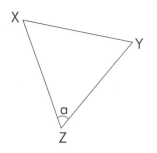

_____

13. Mr. Yang bought 25 bottles of milk. If each bottle contained $\frac{3}{4}$ L of milk, how much milk did Mr. Yang buy?

_____

14. Eight children are standing in different positions shown below. Identify the person who is standing in the northwest.

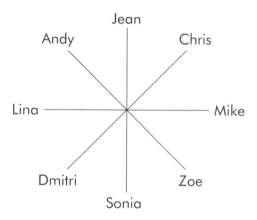

_____

15. Giselle is facing south. If she makes a [   ]° turn in the counterclockwise direction, she will face northeast.

_____

Singapore Math Level 4A & 4B

Solve the following story problems. Show your work in the space below.

16. There were 32 children at a party. There were 8 more boys than girls. If 8 girls wore glasses, what fraction of the girls wore glasses at the party?

17. There were 104 people at a museum. $\frac{3}{8}$ of the people were women. If there were 28 children at the museum, how many men were there?

18. Ana had some money. She used $\frac{4}{7}$ of it to buy a pair of shoes which cost $96. If she spent another $\frac{2}{7}$ of the money to buy a dress, how much did she spend altogether?

Singapore Math Level 4A & 4B

19. Draw an angle of 168° and label it as x.

Look at the picture and fill in each blank with the correct answer.

20.

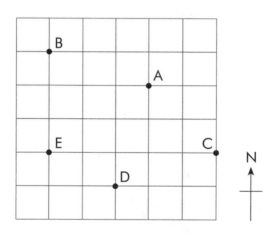

(a) Letter A is _____ of letter B.

(b) Letter B is _____ of letter E.

(c) Letter C is _____ of letter D.

(d) Letter E is _____ of letter D.

(e) Letter E is _____ of letter C.

Singapore Math Level 4A & 4B

Unit 7: PERPENDICULAR AND PARALLEL LINES

Examples:

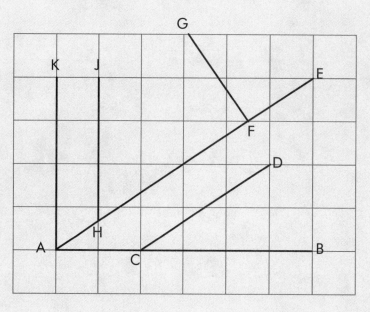

1. Identify all the perpendicular lines.

   KA ⊥ AB and **GF ⊥ HE**

2. Identify all the parallel lines.

   HE // CD and **KA // JH**

3. Identify all vertical lines.

   KA and **JH**

4. Identify all horizontal lines.

   AB

Singapore Math Level 4A & 4B

1. Draw a line perpendicular to the line AB through the point Z.

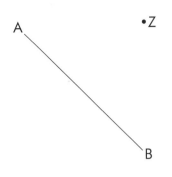

2. Draw a line perpendicular to the line CD through the point Y.

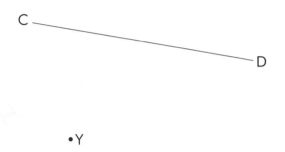

3. (a) Draw a line perpendicular to the line EF through the point X.

    (b) Draw a line perpendicular to the line EF through the point Y.

• X

E ———————————————————————— F

• Y

83

4. (a) Draw a line perpendicular to line GH through the point A.

(b) Draw a line perpendicular to line GH through the point B.

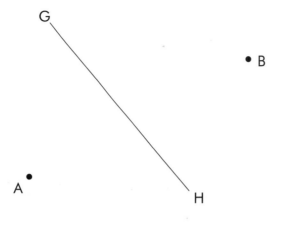

5. Draw a line parallel to MN through the point S.

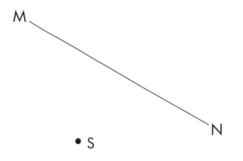

6. Draw a pair of parallel lines through the points V and W.

• V

• W

7.   (a)   Draw a line parallel to AB through the point X.

      (b)   Draw a line parallel to AB through the point Y.

Y
•

A ———————————————————— B

X
•

8.

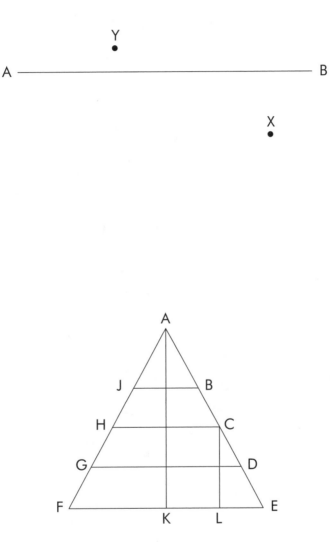

(a)   Identify all pairs of parallel lines in the figure above.

_____

(b)   Identify all pairs of perpendicular lines in the figure above.

_____

9. The figure below shows a section of a brick wall.

   (a) Draw a vertical line through A to meet XY and label it as AB.

   (b) Draw a horizontal line through A and label it as AC.

10. The figure below shows a rectangular fish tank.

   (a) Identify all the horizontal lines. _____

   (b) Identify all the vertical lines. _____

11. The figure on the right shows a box.

   (a) Line AB is a _____ line.

   (b) Line BC is a _____ line.

   (c) Line DC is a _____ line.

   (d) Line AD is a _____ line.

Singapore Math Level 4A & 4B

Unit 8: RECTANGLES AND SQUARES

Examples:

1. Is this figure a rectangle or a square? List one property.

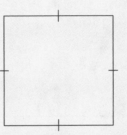

This figure is a square.

It has four sides. / All four sides are equal. / It has two pairs of parallel lines. / All four angles are right angles.

2. The figure below is made up of a rectangle and a square.

   (a) Find the length of AG.

   (b) Find the length of CE.

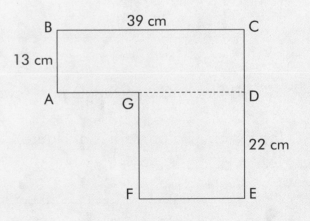

   (a) FE = 22 cm

   AG = 39 – 22 = **17 cm**

   (b) CE = 13 + 22 = **35 cm**

Singapore Math Level 4A & 4B

Look at the figures below.

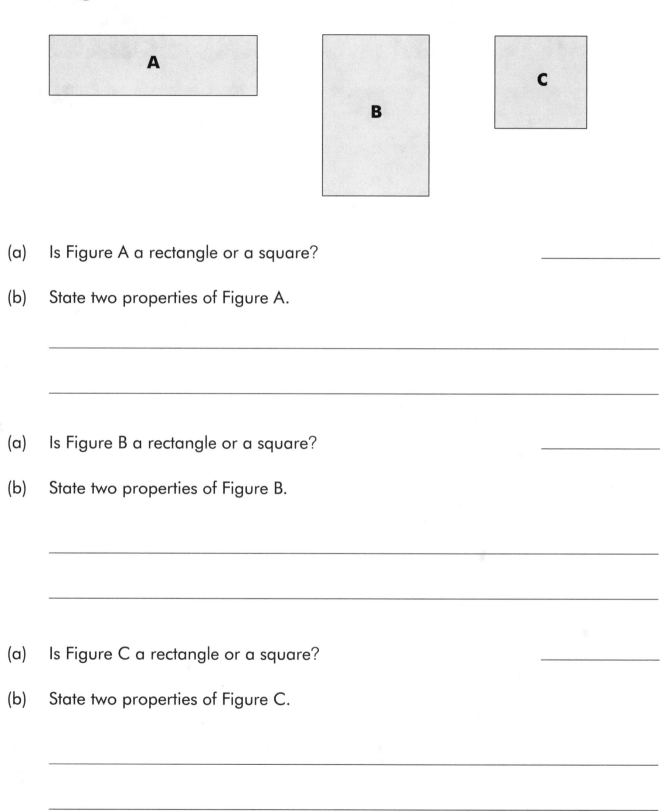

1. (a)   Is Figure A a rectangle or a square?   _____

    (b)   State two properties of Figure A.

    _____

    _____

2. (a)   Is Figure B a rectangle or a square?   _____

    (b)   State two properties of Figure B.

    _____

    _____

3. (a)   Is Figure C a rectangle or a square?   _____

    (b)   State two properties of Figure C.

    _____

    _____

Singapore Math Level 4A & 4B

4. Draw Figure X in the box based on the given hints.

- It has four equal sides.
- It has two pairs of parallel lines.
- It has four right angles.

5. Draw Figure Z in the box based on the given hints.

- It has four sides.
- It has two pairs of parallel lines.
- It has equal opposite sides.

6. Find the unknown sides.

x = _____ in.

y = _____ in.

Singapore Math Level 4A & 4B

7. If the length of the figure below is five times its width, find the unknown sides.

40 cm

x

y

x = _____ cm

y = _____ cm

8. Find the unknown sides.

10 ft.

x

y

x = _____ ft.

y = _____ ft.

9. The figure below is not drawn to scale. Find the unknown marked angle.

z

15°

$\angle z$ = _____°

10. The figure below is not drawn to scale. Find the unknown marked angle.

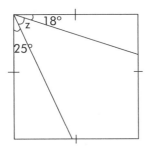

z   18°

25°

$\angle z$ = _____°

Singapore Math Level 4A & 4B

11. The figure below is not drawn to scale. Find the unknown marked angle.

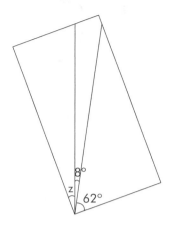

$\angle z = \underline{\hspace{2cm}}^\circ$

12. The figure below is not drawn to scale. Find the unknown marked angle.

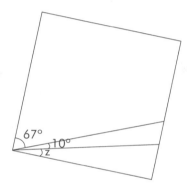

$\angle z = \underline{\hspace{2cm}}^\circ$

13. The figure below is not drawn to scale. Find the unknown marked angle.

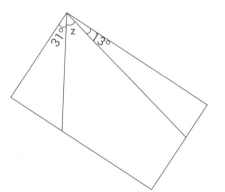

$\angle z = \underline{\hspace{2cm}}^\circ$

Singapore Math Level 4A & 4B

14. The figure below is made up of two rectangles. Find AB and AH.

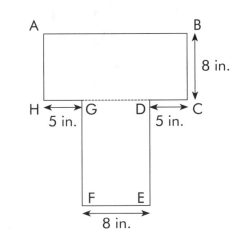

15. The figure below is made up of two identical squares and a rectangle. Find DF and EF.

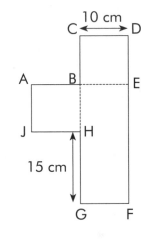

16. The figure below is made up of three rectangles. Find EF and DE.

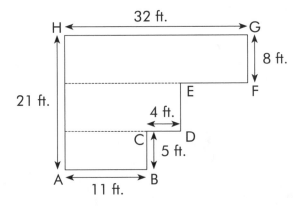

Singapore Math Level 4A & 4B

17. The figure below is made up of a big rectangle and two small identical rectangles. Find ML and AB.

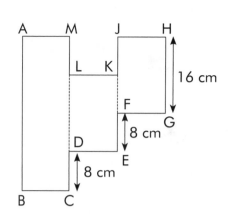

18. The figure below is made up of two rectangles and a square. Find BC and EF.

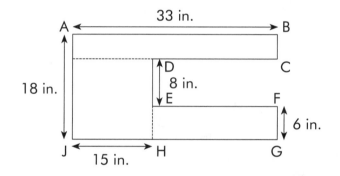

REVIEW 4

Choose the correct answer. Write its number in the parentheses.

1. Which of the following lines shows a vertical line?

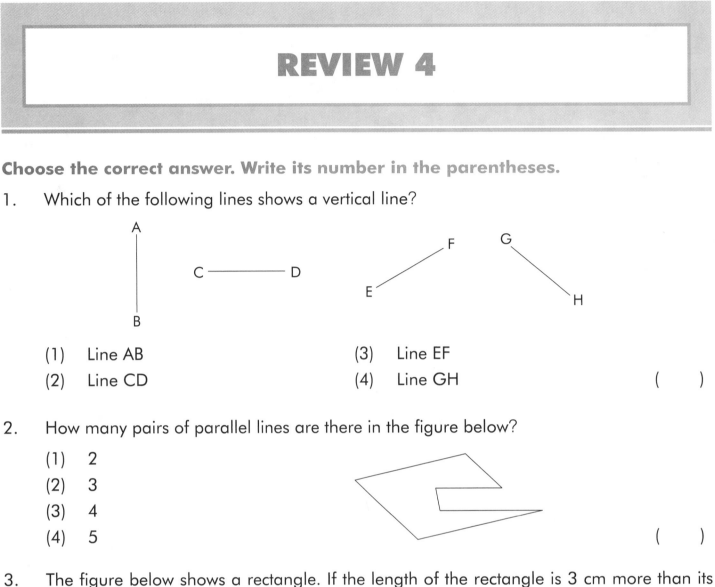

   (1) Line AB   (3) Line EF
   (2) Line CD   (4) Line GH   (   )

2. How many pairs of parallel lines are there in the figure below?
   (1) 2
   (2) 3
   (3) 4
   (4) 5   (   )

3. The figure below shows a rectangle. If the length of the rectangle is 3 cm more than its width, find x.
   (1) 14 cm
   (2) 15 cm
   (3) 18 cm
   (4) 20 cm   (   )

   17 cm

   x

4. The figure below is not drawn to scale. Find the unknown marked angle in the figure below.
   (1) 16°
   (2) 42°
   (3) 64°
   (4) 106°   (   )

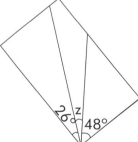

Singapore Math Level 4A & 4B

The figure below is made up of two identical squares and two identical rectangles. Use this figure to answer questions 5 and 6.

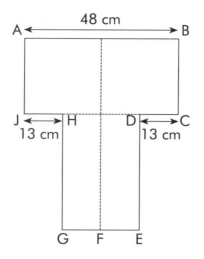

5.   Find the length of AJ.

    (1)   12 cm   (3)   24 cm

    (2)   22 cm   (4)   35 cm   (   )

6.   Find the length of FE.

    (1)   35 cm   (3)   11 cm

    (2)   22 cm   (4)   10 cm   (   )

For questions 7 and 8, refer to the figure below.

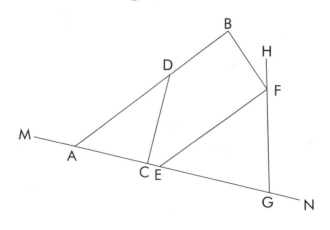

7.   Which line is perpendicular to MN?

    (1)   BA   (3)   FE

    (2)   DC   (4)   HG   (   )

Singapore Math Level 4A & 4B

8. Which line is parallel to AB?

    (1)   BF   (3)   EF

    (2)   CD   (4)   GH   (   )

9. How many lines are parallel to Line XY in the figure below?

    (1)   2

    (2)   3

    (3)   4

    (4)   5   (   )

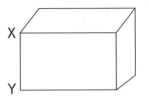

10. How many horizontal lines are there in the figure below?

    (1)   2

    (2)   3

    (3)   4

    (4)   6   (   )

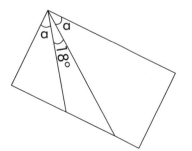

Write your answers on the lines.

11. Identify a line perpendicular to line XY.

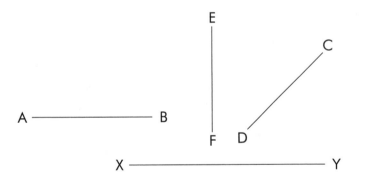

_____

12. The figure below is not drawn to scale. Find the unknown marked angle.

_____

Singapore Math Level 4A & 4B

13. State one property of the figure shown below.

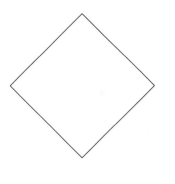

_____

14. The figure below is made up of two identical rectangles. Find line AF.

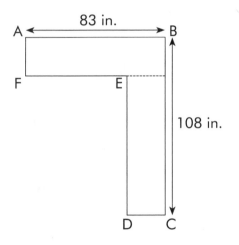

_____

15. Identify two parallel lines in the figure shown below.

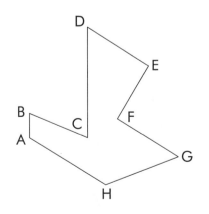

_____

Use the following figure to answer questions 16 and 17.

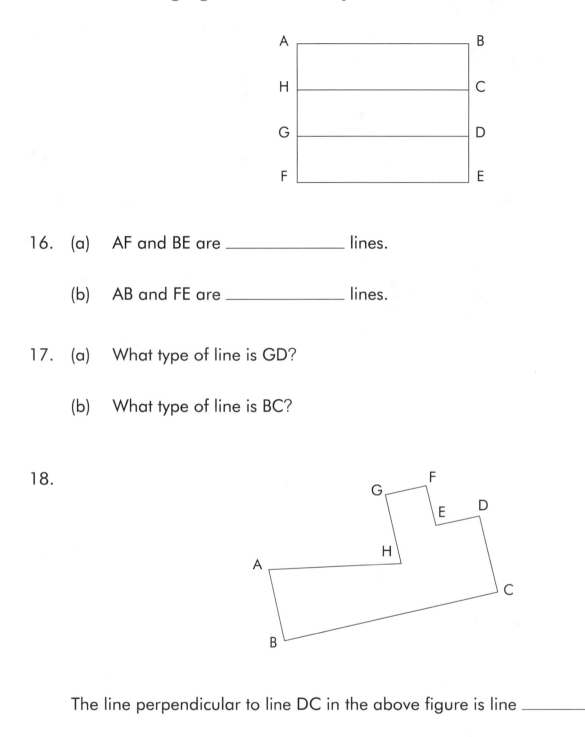

16. (a)   AF and BE are _____ lines.

    (b)   AB and FE are _____ lines.

17. (a)   What type of line is GD?   _____

    (b)   What type of line is BC?   _____

18.

The line perpendicular to line DC in the above figure is line _____.

19. Draw a figure based on the given hints.

- It has two pairs of parallel lines.

- It has four sides.

20. Draw a line that is parallel to GH.

Singapore Math Level 4A & 4B

MID-REVIEW

Choose the correct answer. Write its number in the parentheses.

1. 1,500 more than 86,576 is _____.

   (1) 85,026   (3) 87,581

   (2) 85,076   (4) 88,076   (   )

2. The digit 0 in 13,095 is in the _____ place.

   (1) ten thousands   (3) hundreds

   (2) thousands   (4) tens   (   )

3. Forty-five thousand, forty written in numeral is _____.

   (1) 45,014   (3) 45,140

   (2) 45,040   (4) 45,400   (   )

4. Which of the following is **not** a factor of 66?

   (1) 2   (3) 8

   (2) 3   (4) 11   (   )

5. Which of the following is 9,000 when rounded to the nearest ten?

   (1) 8,990   (3) 9,004

   (2) 8,994   (4) 9,009   (   )

6. $3\frac{2}{5} = \frac{\square}{5}$. The missing number in the box is _____.

   (1) 7   (3) 15

   (2) 10   (4) 17   (   )

Singapore Math Level 4A & 4B

7. $3{,}904 \times 8 = $ _____

    (1) 30,232   (3) 31,520

    (2) 31,232   (4) 32,520   (   )

8. How many quarters are there in $5\frac{3}{4}$?

    (1) 15   (3) 20

    (2) 19   (4) 23   (   )

9. A movie theater sold 1,659 tickets on Thursday and three times as many tickets on Friday. How many tickets did it sell on both days?

    (1) 3,318   (3) 6,636

    (2) 4,977   (4) 8,295   (   )

10. Anya spent $40 and had $10 left. What fraction of her money did she spend?

    (1) $\frac{1}{5}$ (3) $\frac{3}{4}$

    (2) $\frac{1}{4}$ (4) $\frac{4}{5}$ (   )

The following table shows Lily's grades in four subjects. Study it carefully and answer questions 11 and 12.

Subject	English	Math	Science	Social studies
Grade	75	90	63	81

11. What was the total score for Lily's best three subjects?

    (1) 219   (3) 234

    (2) 228   (4) 246   (   )

12. What was the difference between the highest and the lowest scores?

    (1) 9   (3) 18

    (2) 15   (4) 27   (   )

13. How many pair(s) of perpendicular lines are in the figure below?

   (1) 1
   (2) 2
   (3) 3
   (4) 4

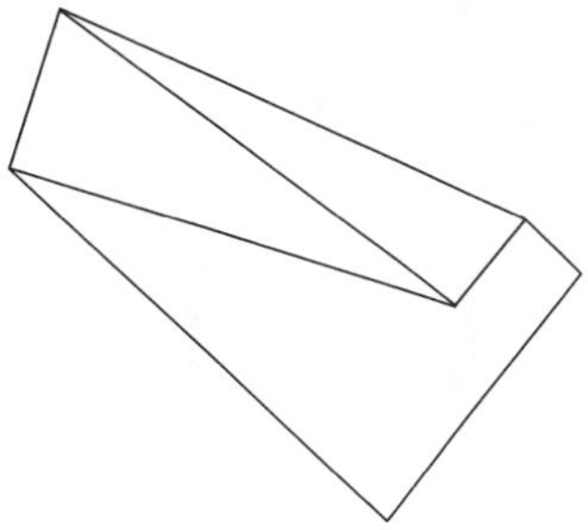

   (   )

14. Charlotte is facing north. If she turns counterclockwise 225°, she will be facing _____.

   (1) northeast   (3) northwest
   (2) southeast   (4) southwest   (   )

15. Find ∠m with the use of a protractor.

   (1) 55°
   (2) 60°
   (3) 115°
   (4) 120°   (   )

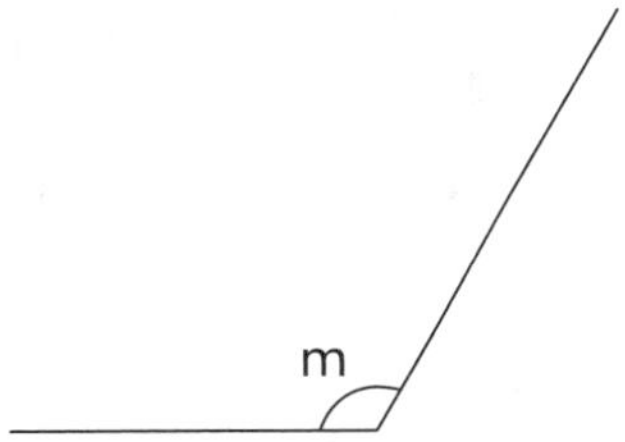

16. Which of the following is the third multiple of 8?

   (1) 16   (3) 26
   (2) 24   (4) 28   (   )

17. The figure below is made up of a rectangle and a square. Find QR.

   (1) 10 yd.
   (2) 12 yd.
   (3) 15 yd.
   (4) 18 yd.

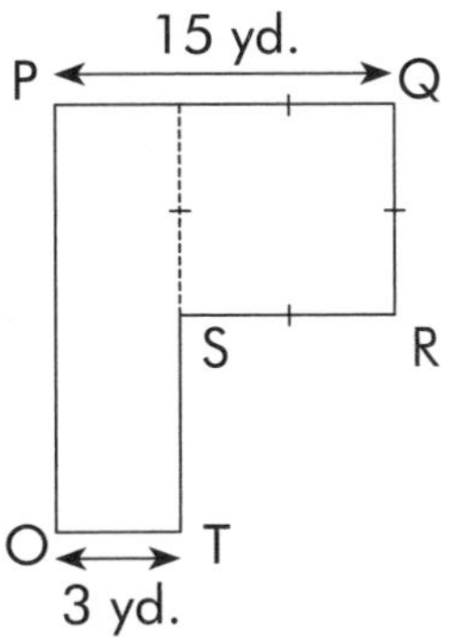

   (   )

Singapore Math Level 4A & 4B

18. 14 thousands more than 58,750 is _____.

    (1)   44,750   (3)   58,764

    (2)   58,736   (4)   72,750   (   )

19. $1,489 \div 8 =$ _____ R _____

    (1)   185, 1   (3)   186, 1

    (2)   185, 6   (4)   186, 5   (   )

20. Which of the following shows an angle of 85°?

    (1)   (3)

    (2)   (4)

                                                                (   )

Write your answers on the lines.

21. 2 ten thousands + 5 thousands + 31 hundreds + 6 tens + 4 ones = ☐

    Write the correct answer in numeral form.

                                                                         _____

22. Complete the number pattern.

    35,070, ☐, 35,230, 35,310, 35,390   _____

23. $180° =$ ☐ –turn   _____

24. Find the product of 532 and 37.   _____

25. 21 and 42 are the first two common multiples of ☐ and ☐.

                                                                         _____

Singapore Math Level 4A & 4B

26. Write $\frac{58}{6}$ as a mixed number in its simplest form.   _____

27. Measure $\angle x$.

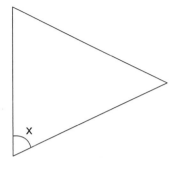

                                                              _____

28. Draw a line perpendicular to CD through the point X.

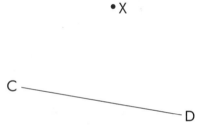

29. WXYZ is a square. It is not drawn to scale. Find $\angle a$ and $\angle b$.

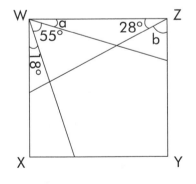

                                                              $\angle a =$ _____

                                                              $\angle b =$ _____

30. Find the value of $3 + \frac{2}{5} + \frac{9}{10}$.   _____

Singapore Math Level 4A & 4B

31. Based on the given hints, write 'Nicholas' and 'Zoe' in the correct boxes.

- Nicholas is standing north of Susie.
- Zoe is standing southwest of Susie.

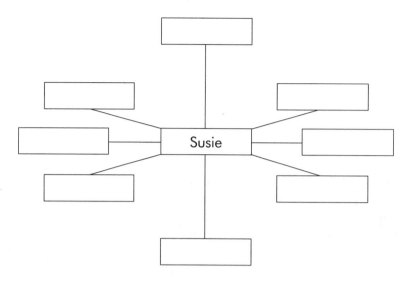

32. Fill in each box with the correct answer.

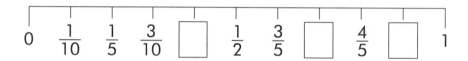

For questions 33 and 34, study the table below. It shows the number of pots of flowers sold by a florist during a five-day fair.

Monday	ЖЖ ЖЖ ЖЖ I
Tuesday	ЖЖ ЖЖ II
Wednesday	ЖЖ ЖЖ ЖЖ III
Thursday	ЖЖ ЖЖ ЖЖ ЖЖ
Friday	ЖЖ ЖЖ ЖЖ ЖЖ IIII

Singapore Math Level 4A & 4B

33. Use the data from the previous table to complete the following table.

Day	Number of pots of flowers
Monday	
Tuesday	
Wednesday	
Thursday	
Friday	

34. How many pots of flowers did the florist sell in all? _____

35. Estimate the value of 421 ÷ 8. _____

36. How many right angles are there in the figure below?

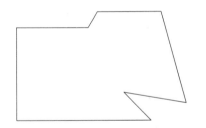

_____

37. When a number is divided by 7, it has a quotient of 26 and a remainder of 5. What is the number?

_____

38. Mrs. Takashi bought 12 lb. of flour. She used $\frac{5}{6}$ of it to bake some pies. How much flour does she have left?

_____

39. $9,055 \times 7 \approx$ ☐ _____

Singapore Math Level 4A & 4B

40. Draw an angle measuring 270°.

Solve the following story problems. Show your work in the space below.

41. Mr. Fay saved $630 a month for eight months. He then bought a television set and a stereo. After paying $295 for the stereo, he had $1,853 left. What was the cost of the television set?

42. A soccer ball costs $15 more than a book. A remote-controlled car costs $198 more than the soccer ball. If the remote-controlled car costs $230, what is the cost of the book?

Singapore Math Level 4A & 4B

43. Alex, Juan, and Cindy shared a pizza. Alex ate $\frac{1}{4}$ of it. Brandon ate $\frac{1}{8}$ of the pizza more than Alex, and Cindy ate the rest of the pizza. What fraction of the pizza did Cindy eat?

44. Esther had 56 stickers. She gave $\frac{3}{8}$ of them to her sister. She gave some stickers to her friend. If she had 18 stickers left, how many stickers did she give to her friend?

45. Mr. Popovic is 76 years old and his granddaughter is 12 years old this year. In how many years will Mr. Popovic be five times as old as his granddaughter?

Singapore Math Level 4A & 4B

CHALLENGE QUESTIONS

Solve the following questions on another sheet of paper.

1. The number of eggs sold by Mrs. Bowles was observed in the pattern shown below.
   Fill in each box with the correct answer.

Day	1	2	3	4	5	6	7	8
Number of eggs sold	15	25		48	61		90	

2. Shani is four times as old as Jenny. Jenny is 3 years older than Enrique. If their total age is 57, how old will Jenny be in four years?

3. When I divide Number A by Number B, the answer is $6\frac{1}{4}$. If Number A is less than 30 and Number B is less than 10, what are numbers A and B?

4. I am a 5-digit number. My first digit is 2 more than the last digit but 2 less than my second digit. My second digit is the third multiple of 3, while my fourth digit is the second multiple of 3. My third digit is the difference between my second and fourth digits. What number am I?

5. The product of numbers X and Y is 600. The sum of the two numbers is 50. What are numbers X and Y?

6. Chet scored six times higher than Hugo on an English test. Jason's score on the same test was the sixth multiple of 10. If the three boys scored a total of 172, what was Chet's score on the test?

7. The difference of two numbers is 132. When one of the numbers is divided by the other, the quotient is 12. What are the two numbers?

Singapore Math Level 4A & 4B

8. Mieke wants to buy a bag. She saves $2 the first week. She saves $4 the second week. She saves $6 the third week and so on. In order to buy the bag, she needs to save for 8 weeks at this pattern. How much does the bag cost?

9. I am a 4-digit number. All my digits are factors of 8. The product of the first and last digits is the fourth multiple of 8. The second digit is 3 less than the last digit. If the first digit is the largest number, what number am I?

10. Place the first six multiples of 6 in each box so that the sum of each row is equal to the 10th and 11th multiples of 6.

| | | | 10th multiple of 6 |
| | | | 11th multiple of 6 |

11. Mr. Garza earns twice as much as his wife. Mrs. Garza earns twice as much as her sister. If Mrs. Garza's sister earns $1,255 a month, how much do the three of them earn in a year?

12. The clock below shows the time Sylvia wakes up in the morning. When the minute hand turns 150°, Sylvia eats her breakfast. At what time does Sylvia eat her breakfast?

Singapore Math Level 4A & 4B

4B LEARNING OUTCOMES

Unit 9   Decimals (Part 1)
Students should be able to
- recognize place values (tenths, hundredths, and thousandths) in decimals.
- express a fraction as a decimal, and vice versa.
- compare and arrange decimals.
- round decimals to the nearest whole number, 1 decimal place, or 2 decimal places.

Unit 10   Decimals (Part 2)
Students should be able to
- add and subtract decimals.
- multiply and divide decimals.
- estimate the value of decimals.
- check that answers are reasonable.
- solve up to 2-step story problems related to decimals.

Review 5
This review tests students' understanding of Units 9 & 10.

Unit 11   Time
Students should be able to
- count time in seconds.
- write time by separating hours, minutes, and seconds by a colon.
- find the length of 2 different times.
- calculate the starting or ending time given the length of time.

Unit 12   Perimeter and Area
Students should be able to
- calculate perimeter and area of rectangles, squares, and composite figures.
- find length or width of a rectangle/square given its perimeter/area.
- solve story problems related to perimeter and area.

Review 6
This review tests students' understanding of Units 11 & 12.

Unit 13   Symmetry
Students should be able to
- identify symmetrical figures.
- identify the lines of symmetry in figures.
- complete symmetrical figures and patterns.

Unit 14   Tessellations
Students should be able to
- identify shapes that repeat without gaps or overlaps.
- identify the unit shape in tessellations.
- complete tessellations by drawing more unit shapes on dot papers.
- draw unit shapes in tessellations in more than one way.

Review 7
This review tests students' understanding of Units 13 & 14.

Final Review
This review is an excellent assessment of students' understanding of all the topics in this book.

FORMULA SHEET

Unit 9 Decimals (Part 1)

Word	Decimal	Fraction	
1 tenth	0.1	$\frac{1}{10}$	10 tenths = 1 one
1 hundredth	0.01	$\frac{1}{100}$	100 hundredths = 1 one
1 thousandth	0.001	$\frac{1}{1,000}$	1,000 thousandths = 1 one

Writing decimals
14.925 is **1 ten 4 ones 9 tenths 2 hundredths 5 thousandths**.

Place value
Each digit in a decimal is in a different place and has a different value. The place value will help us identify the digit in a particular place such as thousands, hundreds, tens, ones, tenths, hundredths, or thousandths and its value.

Example: In 43.082,
   the digit 3 is in the **ones** place.
   the digit 2 stands for **2 thousandths** or **0.002**.
   the value of the digit 8 is **0.08**.

More than and *Less than*
The term *more than* means addition (+).
The term *less than* means subtraction (−).

Comparing decimals
1. Compare the whole numbers (thousands, hundreds, tens, and ones) first.
2. Next, compare the tenths.
3. Then, compare the hundredths.
4. Finally, compare the thousandths.

Order
When arranging a set of decimals in order,
* determine if the order must begin with the greatest or the smallest,
* compare the place value of the decimals,
* arrange the decimals in the correct order.

Rounding decimals
To round a decimal to the nearest whole number, look at the digit in the tenths place.

If the digit in the tenths place is equal to or more than 5, round up to a higher number.

If the digit in the tenths place is less than 5, the whole number will remain as it is.

Examples: $4.7 \approx 5$ $4.1 \approx 4$

To round a decimal to the nearest tenth or 1 decimal place, look at the digit in the hundredths place.

If the digit in the hundredths place is equal to or more than 5, round up to the nearest tenth.

If the digit in the hundredths place is less than 5, the digit in the tenths place will remain.

Examples: $4.76 \approx 4.8$ $4.72 \approx 4.7$

To round a decimal to the nearest hundredth or 2 decimal places, look at the digit in the thousandths place.

If the digit in the thousandths place is equal to or more than 5, round up to the nearest hundredth.

If the digit in the thousandths place is less than 5, the digit in the hundredths place will remain.

Examples: $4.759 \approx 4.76$ $4.783 \approx 4.78$

Alternatively, use a number line as a guide in rounding decimals.

Example:

$$2.5 \quad\quad 2.57 \approx 2.6 \quad\quad 2.6$$

Convert a fraction to a decimal
Make the denominator 10, 100, or 1,000.
Remember to multiply both numerator and denominator with the same number.

Example: $\frac{1 \times 5}{20 \times 5} = \frac{5}{100} = 0.05$

Convert a mixed number to a decimal
* Break down the mixed number into a whole number and a fraction.
* Make the denominator 10, 100, or 1,000
* Convert the fraction to a decimal.

Example: $6\frac{3}{25} = 6 + \frac{3 \times 4}{25 \times 4} = 6 + \frac{12}{100} = 6\frac{12}{100} = 6.12$

Convert a decimal to a fraction
When a decimal has only tenths, the denominator is 10.
When a decimal has only hundredths, the denominator is 100.
When a decimal has only thousandths, the denominator is 1,000.

Example: $0.15 = \frac{15}{100}$

Convert a decimal to a mixed number
* Break down the decimal into a whole number and a decimal.
* Convert the decimal to a fraction.
* Add the fraction to the whole number.
* Write the fraction in its simplest form.

Example: $6.12 = 6 + 0.12 = 6 + \frac{12}{100} = 6\frac{12}{100} = 6\frac{3}{25}$

Unit 10 Decimals (Part 2)

Adding decimals
- Make sure the decimal points are aligned.
- Add the hundredths first. Regroup the tenths if required.
- Add the tenths. Regroup the tenths if required.
- Add the whole numbers. Regroup the whole numbers if required.

Subtracting decimals
- Make sure the decimal points are aligned.
- Subtract the hundredths first. Regroup if required.
- Subtract the tenths. Regroup if required.
- Subtract the whole numbers. Regroup if required.

Multiplying decimals
- Multiply the hundredths by the multiplier. Regroup the hundredths if required.
- Multiply the tenths by the multiplier. Regroup the tenths if required.
- Multiply the whole number by the multiplier. Regroup if required.

Dividing decimals
- Divide the whole number by the divisor. Regroup the remainder if required.
- Divide the tenths by the divisor. Regroup the remainder if required.
- Divide the hundredths by the divisor. There can be a remainder sometimes.

Estimation in decimals
Step 1: Round the numbers to the nearest whole number, the nearest tenth, or the nearest hundredth.
Step 2: Add, subtract, multiply, or divide accordingly.

Unit 11 Time

Seconds

1 minute = 60 seconds
Unit of measurement: sec.

Each number on the clock is equivalent to 5 seconds.
The second hand on the clock is usually longer than the hour and minute hands.

Example: When the second hand moves from 3 to 5 on the face of the clock, it means 2×5 sec. = 10 sec. has passed.

Time can be written by separating hour, minutes, and seconds with a colon.

Example: nine thirty-three and twelve seconds in the morning is 9:33:12 A.M.

You can use a time line to find the duration or a particular time.

Unit 12 Perimeter and Area

Square
A square has four equal sides.
Perimeter = 4 × Length
Area = Length × Length

Rectangle
A rectangle has two pairs of equal sides.

Perimeter = Length + Width + Length + Width
Area = Length × Width

Composite Figures
In order to find the area or perimeter of a composite figure, first separate the figure into rectangle(s) or square(s).

Finding the selected area in a figure

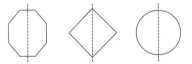

Area of shaded area = Area of big rectangle –
                       Area of small rectangle

Unit 13 Symmetry
A *line of symmetry* is a line that divides a figure into two equal parts. The *line of symmetry* is usually a dotted line.

A symmetrical figure is a figure that can be divided into two equal parts by a line of symmetry.

Some examples of symmetrical figures:

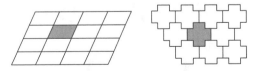

Completing symmetrical shapes or patterns
Step 1: Use the dotted line as the line of symmetry.
Step 2: Trace or shade the other half of the symmetrical shape or pattern accordingly to the first half.

Unit 14 Tessellations
A *tessellation* is a type of pattern that is tiled using a unit shape with no gaps in between.

Examples of tessellations:

A tessellation can be made by using a unit shape on the dot grid. Also, tessellations can be drawn with some shapes in 2 or more ways.

Singapore Math Level 4A & 4B

Unit 9: DECIMALS (PART 1)

Examples:

1. Change $8\frac{37}{100}$ to a decimal.

   $8\frac{37}{100} = 8$ ones 37 hundredths = **8.37**

2. What number is 0.005 more than 6.323?   **6.328**

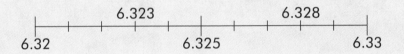

3. Arrange the decimals in order, beginning with the largest.

   0.708   0.078   0.78

   0.78, 0.708, 0.078

4. Round 28.69 to the nearest tenth.

   $28.69 \approx$ **28.7**

Singapore Math Level 4A & 4B

The shaded parts represent the decimals. Write the correct decimals on the lines provided.

1.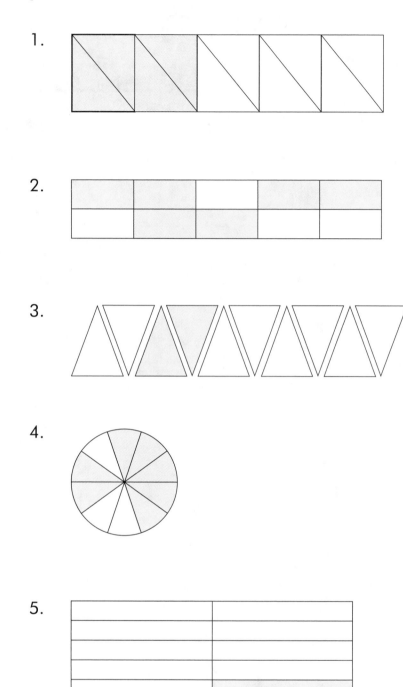

   _____

2. _____

3. _____

4. _____

5. _____

Singapore Math Level 4A & 4B

Write the following in decimals.

6.   7 tenths = _____

7.   3 ones 2 tenths = _____

8.   4 ones 13 tenths = _____

9.   2 ones 18 tenths = _____

10. 9 ones 24 tenths = _____

Write each decimal in tenths.

11. 0.9 = _____ tenths

12. 3.6 = _____ tenths

13. 78.4 = _____ tenths

14. 18.3 = _____ tenths

15. 21.5 = _____ tenths

For each number line, fill in each box with the correct decimal.

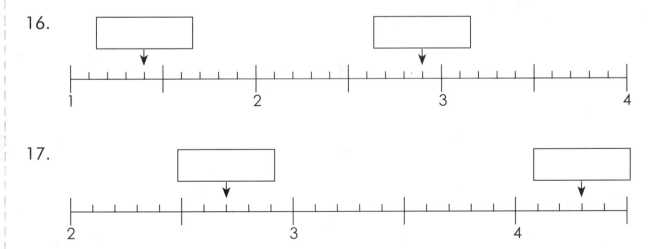

16.

17.

Singapore Math Level 4A & 4B

18.

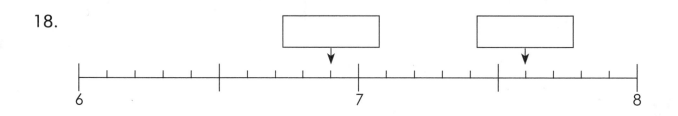

Fill in each blank with the correct answer.

19. 9.1 = _____ ones 1 tenth

20. 42.6 = _____ tens 2 ones 6 tenths

21. 17.3 = 1 ten 7 ones _____ tenths

22. 69.5 = _____ tens 9 ones 5 tenths

23. 82.8 = 8 tens 2 ones _____ tenths

24. In 91.3,

    (a)   the digit _____ is in the ones place.

    (b)   the digit 3 is in the _____ place.

    (c)   the value of the digit 9 is _____.

    (d)   the digit 1 stands for _____.

25. In 57.6,

    (a)   the digit _____ is in the tens place.

    (b)   the digit 6 is in the _____ place.

    (c)   the value of the digit 7 is _____.

    (d)   the digit 5 stands for _____.

For each question, shade the boxes accordingly to show the correct decimal.

26.
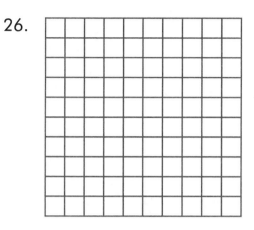
0.26

29.
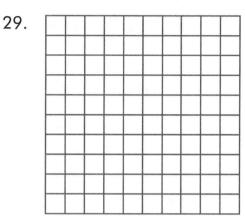
0.62

27.
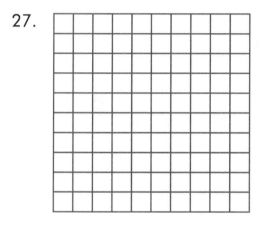
0.74

30.
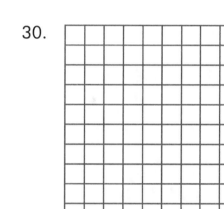
0.45

28.
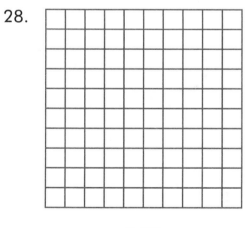
0.03

Write the following in decimals.

31. 8 hundredths = _____

32. 16 hundredths = _____

33. 32 hundredths = _____

34. 188 hundredths = _____

35. 311 hundredths = _____

Write each decimal in hundredths.

36. 5.43 = _____ hundredths

37. 81.95 = _____ hundredths

38. 60.72 = _____ hundredths

39. 38.54 = _____ hundredths

40. 90.45 = _____ hundredths

For each number line, fill in each box with the correct decimal.

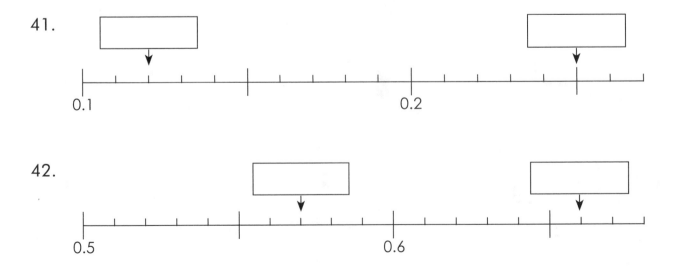

Singapore Math Level 4A & 4B

43.

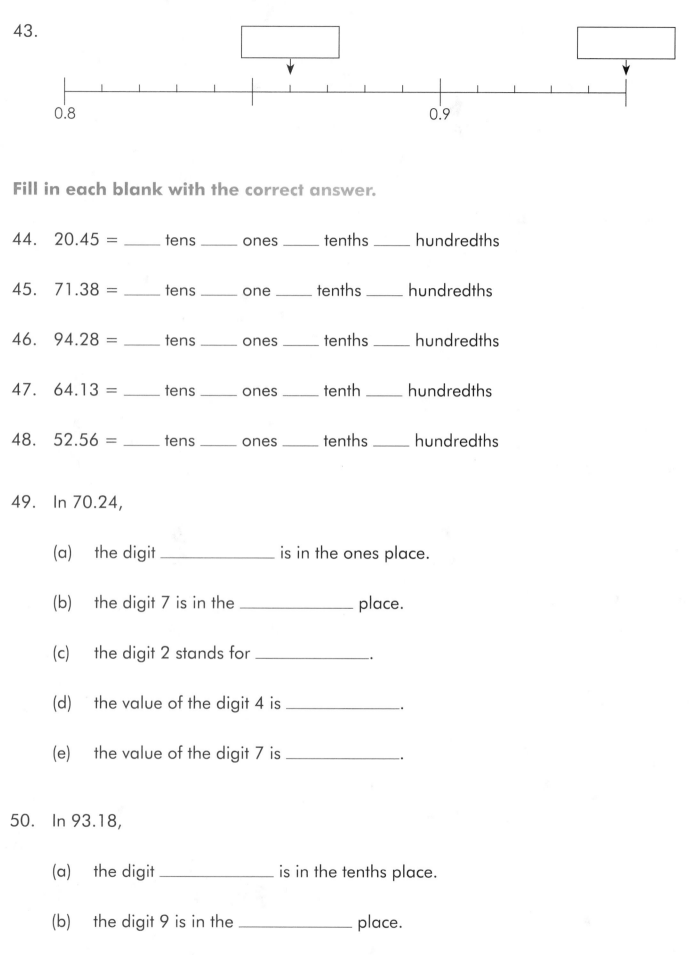

Fill in each blank with the correct answer.

44. 20.45 = _____ tens _____ ones _____ tenths _____ hundredths

45. 71.38 = _____ tens _____ one _____ tenths _____ hundredths

46. 94.28 = _____ tens _____ ones _____ tenths _____ hundredths

47. 64.13 = _____ tens _____ ones _____ tenth _____ hundredths

48. 52.56 = _____ tens _____ ones _____ tenths _____ hundredths

49. In 70.24,

   (a) the digit _____ is in the ones place.

   (b) the digit 7 is in the _____ place.

   (c) the digit 2 stands for _____.

   (d) the value of the digit 4 is _____.

   (e) the value of the digit 7 is _____.

50. In 93.18,

   (a) the digit _____ is in the tenths place.

   (b) the digit 9 is in the _____ place.

Singapore Math Level 4A & 4B

(c)   the digit 3 stands for _____.

(d)   the value of the digit 8 is _____.

(e)   the value of the digit 1 is _____.

Write the following in decimals.

51.   4 thousandths = _____

52.   15 thousandths = _____

53.   291 thousandths = _____

54.   718 thousandths = _____

55.   1,414 thousandths = _____

56.   2,086 thousandths = _____

Write each decimal in thousandths.

57.   28.404 = _____ thousandths

58.   40.687 = _____ thousandths

59.   53.936 = _____ thousandths

60.   2.308 = _____ thousandths

61.   66.799 = _____ thousandths

Singapore Math Level 4A & 4B

For each number line, fill in each box with the correct decimal.

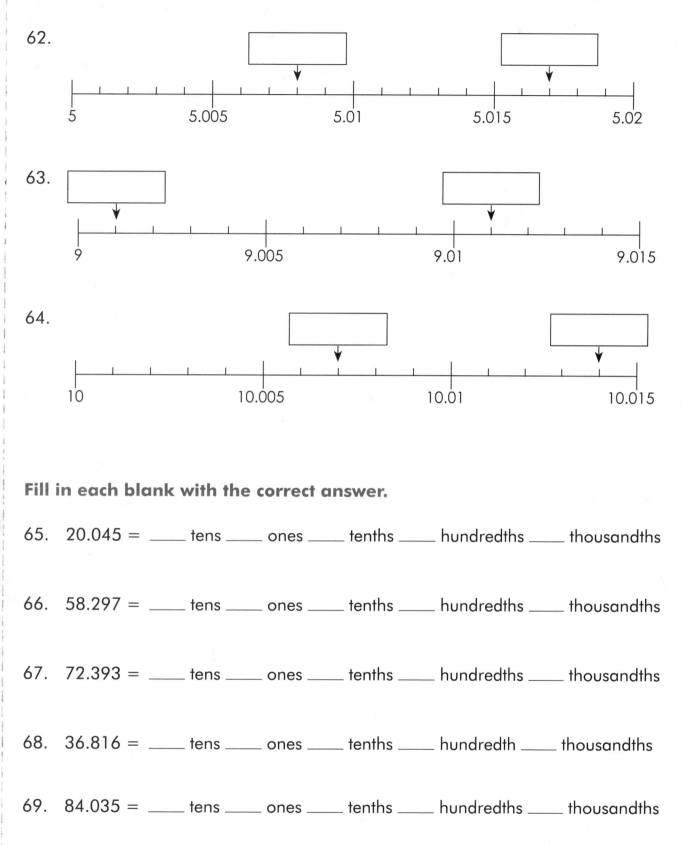

62.

63.

64.

Fill in each blank with the correct answer.

65. 20.045 = _____ tens _____ ones _____ tenths _____ hundredths _____ thousandths

66. 58.297 = _____ tens _____ ones _____ tenths _____ hundredths _____ thousandths

67. 72.393 = _____ tens _____ ones _____ tenths _____ hundredths _____ thousandths

68. 36.816 = _____ tens _____ ones _____ tenths _____ hundredth _____ thousandths

69. 84.035 = _____ tens _____ ones _____ tenths _____ hundredths _____ thousandths

Singapore Math Level 4A & 4B

70. In 4.687,

(a) the digit _____ is in the thousandths place.

(b) the digit 6 is in the _____ place.

(c) the digit 8 stands for _____.

(d) the value of the digit 7 is _____.

(e) the value of the digit 4 is _____.

71. In 10.963,

(a) the digit _____ is in the ones place.

(b) the digit 3 is in the _____ place.

(c) the digit 9 stands for _____.

(d) the value of the digit 1 is _____.

(e) the value of the digit 6 is _____.

72. 0.5 more than 13.9 is _____.

73. 0.02 more than 78.66 is _____.

74. 0.006 less than 85.09 is _____.

75. 0.2 less than 6.7 is _____.

76. 0.01 less than 57.03 is _____.

Singapore Math Level 4A & 4B

Complete the number patterns.

77.   3.8, 4.7, 5.6, _____, _____

78.   15.34, 15.39, 15.44, _____, _____

79.   45.06, 45.09, 45.12, _____, _____

80.   10.088, 10.089, 10.09, _____, _____

81.   82.309, 82.314, 82.319, _____, _____

Circle the largest decimal.

82. 1.28	1.028	1.8	1.208
83. $3\frac{605}{1,000}$	3.65	3.506	$\frac{365}{1,000}$
84. 2.91	$2\frac{901}{1,000}$	$2\frac{9}{100}$	0.291

Circle the smallest decimal.

85. 7.102	7.12	7.021	7.012
86. $8\frac{95}{100}$	8.095	8.905	$\frac{8,059}{1,000}$
87. 3.99	$3\frac{909}{1,000}$	$3\frac{99}{1,000}$	$\frac{399}{1,000}$

Singapore Math Level 4A & 4B

Arrange the decimals in descending order.

88. 5.028,   2.058,   5.28

_____

89. 4.25,   4.025,   4.502

_____

90. 1.09,   9.01,   0.19

_____

Arrange the decimals in ascending order.

91. 198.3,   198.03,   198.003

_____

92. 273.29,   27.329,   2,732.9

_____

93. 6.017,   6.17,   6.107

_____

Round the following decimals to the nearest whole numbers.

94.   1.04   _____

95.   2.55   _____

96.   15.82   _____

97.   0.95   _____

98.   7.74   _____

Round the following decimals to 1 decimal place.

99.   1.68   _____

100.   33.38   _____

101.   2.91   _____

Round the following decimals to the nearest tenth.

102.   14.74   _____

103.   6.472   _____

104.   89.943   _____

Round the following decimals to 2 decimal places.

105.   10.963   _____

106.   59.095   _____

107.   7.007   _____

Singapore Math Level 4A & 4B

Round the following decimals to the nearest hundredths.

108.   0.671   _____

109.   2.386   _____

110.   15.709   _____

Write the following fractions as decimals.

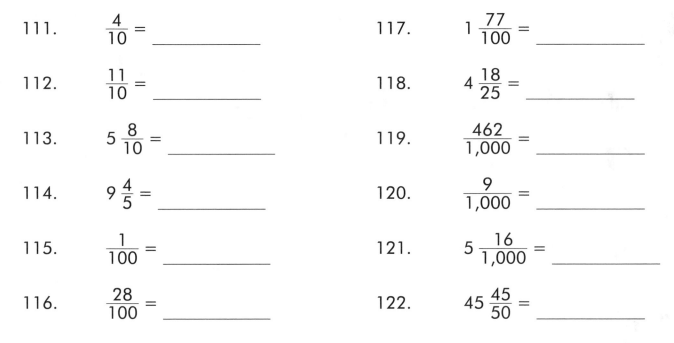

111. $\frac{4}{10}$ = _____

112. $\frac{11}{10}$ = _____

113. $5\frac{8}{10}$ = _____

114. $9\frac{4}{5}$ = _____

115. $\frac{1}{100}$ = _____

116. $\frac{28}{100}$ = _____

117. $1\frac{77}{100}$ = _____

118. $4\frac{18}{25}$ = _____

119. $\frac{462}{1,000}$ = _____

120. $\frac{9}{1,000}$ = _____

121. $5\frac{16}{1,000}$ = _____

122. $45\frac{45}{50}$ = _____

Write each decimal as a fraction or a mixed number in its simplest form.

123.   6.2 = _____

124.   49.4 = _____

125.   7.08 = _____

126.   51.25 = _____

127.   1.008 = _____

128.   25.42 = _____

Singapore Math Level 4A & 4B

Unit 10: DECIMALS (PART 2)

Examples:

1. $3.28 + 4.05 = \underline{\textbf{7.33}}$

$$\begin{array}{r} 3.\overset{1}{2}8 \\ +\ 4.05 \\ \hline 7.33 \end{array}$$

2. $5.94 - 2.31 = \underline{\textbf{3.63}}$

$$\begin{array}{r} 5.94 \\ -\ 2.31 \\ \hline 3.63 \end{array}$$

3. $9.4 \times 6 = \underline{\textbf{56.4}}$

$$\begin{array}{r} \overset{2}{9}.4 \\ \times\quad 6 \\ \hline 56.4 \end{array}$$

4. $15.3 \div 5 = \underline{\textbf{3.06}}$

$$\begin{array}{r} 3.06 \\ 5\overline{\smash{)}15.3} \\ \underline{15} \\ 3 \\ \underline{0} \\ 30 \\ \underline{30} \\ 0 \end{array}$$

5. Estimate 2.91×6.

    $2.91 \times 6 \approx 3 \times 6 = \underline{\textbf{18}}$

Singapore Math Level 4A & 4B

Solve the addition problems below.

1.
```
      0 . 1
  +   0 . 3
  _____
```

4.
```
      5 . 1 4
  + 1 3 . 6 3
  _____
```

2.
```
      6 . 2
  +   1 . 3
  _____
```

5.
```
    5 6 . 0 1
  + 7 2 . 9 6
  _____
```

3.
```
      9 . 0 8
  +   5 . 5 7
  _____
```

6.
```
    3 9 . 7 8
  + 4 4 . 0 5
  _____
```

Solve the subtraction problems below.

7.
```
    0 . 5
 -  0 . 2
_____
```

10.
```
   2 1 . 7 5
 -  8 . 0 3
_____
```

8.
```
    9 . 7
 -  5 . 4
_____
```

11.
```
   9 7 . 3 6
 - 5 0 . 7 2
_____
```

9.
```
    4 . 6 1
 -  2 . 3 9
_____
```

12.
```
   8 0 . 4 9
 - 3 1 . 6 7
_____
```

Singapore Math Level 4A & 4B

Solve the multiplication problems below.

13.
$$\begin{array}{r} 5\,.\,1 \\ \times \quad 2 \\ \hline \end{array}$$

18.
$$\begin{array}{r} 3\,.\,4\;5 \\ \times \qquad 3 \\ \hline \end{array}$$

14.
$$\begin{array}{r} 0\,.\,4 \\ \times \quad 5 \\ \hline \end{array}$$

19.
$$\begin{array}{r} 0\,.\,7\;8 \\ \times \qquad 9 \\ \hline \end{array}$$

15.
$$\begin{array}{r} 3\,.\,8 \\ \times \quad 4 \\ \hline \end{array}$$

20.
$$\begin{array}{r} 1\;2\,.\,3\;6 \\ \times \qquad 5 \\ \hline \end{array}$$

16.
$$\begin{array}{r} 2\,.\,3 \\ \times \quad 6 \\ \hline \end{array}$$

21.
$$\begin{array}{r} 5\;0\,.\,1\;2 \\ \times \qquad 2 \\ \hline \end{array}$$

17.
$$\begin{array}{r} 8\,.\,1\;7 \\ \times \qquad 7 \\ \hline \end{array}$$

22.
$$\begin{array}{r} 2\;1\,.\,5\;5 \\ \times \qquad 6 \\ \hline \end{array}$$

Singapore Math Level 4A & 4B

Solve the division problems below.

23. $3\overline{)7.8}$

27. $9\overline{)27.45}$

24. $5\overline{)5.25}$

28. $4\overline{)43.4}$

25. $2\overline{)4.89}$

29. $9\overline{)812.7}$

26. $4\overline{)16.4}$

30. $6\overline{)402.15}$

135

31. $5\overline{)18}$

32. $8\overline{)10}$

33. Estimate the value of each of the following by first rounding the number to the nearest whole number. Then, decode the message below.

A $26.54 + 92.88 =$ _____

C $84.05 - 77.13 =$ _____

D $5.4 \times 8 =$ _____

E $11.99 \div 3 =$ _____

I $125.09 + 68.01 =$ _____

L $524.87 - 128.39 =$ _____

M $44.19 \times 5 =$ _____

S $35.59 \div 6 =$ _____

40	4	7	193	220	120	397	6

Singapore Math Level 4A & 4B

Solve the following story problems. Show your work in the space below.

34. Mrs. Abdul bought 2.4 lb. of meat. Mrs. Davidson bought 1.35 lb. of meat more than her. How many pounds of meat did they buy altogether?

35. Joan had $108.25. She spent $43.05 to buy a present for her mother and $12.20 on cab fare. How much money did she have left?

Singapore Math Level 4A & 4B

36. A bag of rice and two identical bags of sugar have a mass of 6 kg. The bag of rice and a bag of sugar have a mass of 4.5 kg. Find the mass of five bags of sugar.

37. A train traveled 180.63 mi. on Monday. It traveled 2.1 mi. more on Tuesday than on Monday. It traveled 1.2 mi. less on Wednesday than on Tuesday. What was the distance traveled by the train on Wednesday?

38. Lily has a mass of 24.3 kg. The mass of her father is 3 times as heavy as Lily. What is the total mass of Lily and her father?

39. A ribbon is 21.75 yd. long. Wang cuts two pieces of ribbon measuring a total of 2.4 yd. from it. The remaining piece of ribbon is then cut into three equal pieces. What is the length of each of the three pieces of ribbon?

Singapore Math Level 4A & 4B

40. A box of chocolates costs $11.45. Marcus bought three boxes of chocolates. If he gave the cashier a fifty-dollar bill, how much change would he receive?

41. Mr. Mendoza needed 12.76 gal. of paint to paint a room.

(a) How much paint would he need if he wanted to paint three similar rooms?

(b) If a gallon of paint cost $5, how much money did Mr. Jackson pay for the paint?

Singapore Math Level 4A & 4B

42. Mr. Woods had a bag of sugar. He sold 38.25 kg of it and packed the rest equally into six bags. If each bag of sugar had a mass of 0.75 kg, how much sugar did Mr. Woods have in the beginning?

43. Taylor bought 2 bottles of orange juice and a bottle of apple juice for $6.55. The bottle of apple juice cost $0.35 less than the bottle of orange juice. What was the cost of the bottle of orange juice?

REVIEW 5

Choose the correct answer. Write its number in the parentheses.

1. In 372.48, the digit 8 is in the _____ place.

    (1)   ones   (3)   hundredths

    (2)   tenths   (4)   thousandths   (   )

2. Express $\frac{2}{5}$ as a decimal.

    (1)   0.25   (3)   0.5

    (2)   0.4   (4)   2.5   (   )

3. Find the sum of 5.98 and 1.93.

    (1)   4.05   (3)   7.91

    (2)   6.39   (4)   8.91   (   )

4. Express 62.458 in thousandths.

    (1)   624.58 thousandths   (3)   62,458 thousandths

    (2)   6,245.8 thousandths   (4)   624,580 thousandths   (   )

5. Round 37.46 to 1 decimal place.

    (1)   37.0   (3)   37.5

    (2)   37.4   (4)   38.0   (   )

6. 288.63 ÷ 9 = _____

    (1)   3.207   (3)   32.7

    (2)   32.07   (4)   320.7   (   )

Singapore Math Level 4A & 4B

7. Estimate the value of 12.99 + 5.5 by rounding each number to the nearest whole number first.

   (1)   17   (3)   19
   (2)   18   (4)   20   (   )

Write your answers on the lines.

8. 5 hundreds, 4 tens, 7 tenths, and 1 thousandth written in numerals is [   ].

   _____

9. Write 1.68 as a mixed number in its simplest form.   _____

10. In 89.437, the value of the digit 4 is [   ].   _____

11. $9 \frac{35}{100} = 9 +$ [   ]

   Write your answer as a decimal.   _____

12. Jar A contains 1.9 gallons of water. Jar B contains 2.1 gallons of water and Jar C contains 1.2 gallons of water. What is the total volume of water in the three jugs? Write your answer as a decimal.

   _____

13. Find the product of 1.92 and 8. Round your answer to the nearest tenth.

   _____

14. 305.419 = 3 hundreds 5 ones 4 tenths [   ] thousandths

   _____

Singapore Math Level 4A & 4B

15. Arrange the following decimals in descending order.

    5.06   0.56   5.6   5.006

    _____

16. Katrina has a ribbon 3.78 m long. The length of her ribbon is 3 times as long as Sarah's ribbon. How much longer is Katrina's ribbon than Sarah's ribbon?

    _____

17. Mrs. Cho bought 2.76 lb. of grapes and divided the grapes equally among three neighbors and herself. How much did each person get?

    _____

Solve the following story problems. Show your work in the space below.

18. Elsie travels 12.9 mi. from her house to her office every day. She travels the same distance back home. What is the total distance traveled by Elsie from Monday to Friday?

Singapore Math Level 4A & 4B

19. A boutique paid $2,954.10 to its supplier for 12 similar dresses and 7 similar blouses. If all the dresses cost $2,376.60, how much did each blouse cost?

20. Sheila used 3.6 m of cloth from a 10-m cloth to sew two similar blouses. The remaining cloth was used to sew four identical skirts. How much cloth did Sheila use to sew each skirt?

Singapore Math Level 4A & 4B

146

Unit 11: TIME

Examples:

1. Draw the missing minute and second hands on the clock shown on the right.

30 sec. later

2. Write the time two thirty and twenty-five seconds in the afternoon by separating hours, minutes, and seconds with a colon.

    2:30:25 P.M.

3. Noel started reading a book at 12:56 P.M. She finished reading the book at 2:05 P.M. How long did she take to read the book?

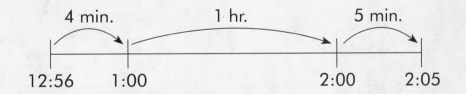

1 hr. + 4 min. + 5 min. = 1 hr. 9 min.

She took **1 hr. 9 min.** to read the book.

Singapore Math Level 4A & 4B

Write the correct length of time on the lines.

1.

James took _____ sec. to get out of his bed.

2.

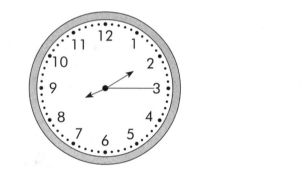 

James took _____ sec. to wash his hands.

3.

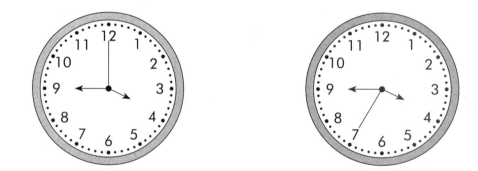

James took _____ sec. to walk from his room to the kitchen.

Singapore Math Level 4A & 4B

4.

James took _____ sec. to pick a piece of paper from the floor.

5.

James took _____ sec. to wash his spoon and fork.

Draw the missing minute and second hands on each clock shown on the right.

6.   Leyla took 40 sec. to read a sentence in her book.

7. Angie took 20 sec. to draw an apple.

8. Andre took 60 sec. to walk to the garden.

9. Jessica took 15 sec. to color a square.

Singapore Math Level 4A & 4B

10.   Leo took 55 sec. to wash two plates.

Write the expected time.

11.   It is 5:34:21 P.M.

 What time will it be in 1 hr. 3 min. 45 sec.?   _____

12.   It is 10:55:47 A.M.

 What time will it be in 2 hr. 6 min. 34 sec.?   _____

13.   It is 8:20:39 P.M.

 What time will it be in 8 hr. 19 min. 54 sec.?   _____

14.   It is 6:41:36 A.M.

 What time will it be in 7 hr. 49 min. 20 sec.?   _____

15.   It is 12:02:59 P.M.

 What time will it be in 0 hr. 59 min. 59 sec.?   _____

Singapore Math Level 4A & 4B

Write the elapsed time.

16. It is 11:27:06 A.M.

    What time was it 6 hr. 42 min. 42 sec. ago? _____

17. It is 3:28:15 P.M.

    What time was it 4 hr. 22 min. 10 sec. ago? _____

18. It is 7:19:21 A.M.

    What time was it 10 hr. 11 min. 8 sec. ago? _____

19. It is 10:44:30 P.M.

    What time was it 5 hr. 53 min. 25 sec. ago? _____

20. It is 2:08:16 A.M.

    What time was it 3 hr. 39 min. 14 sec. ago? _____

For each time line, fill in each blank with the correct answer.

21.

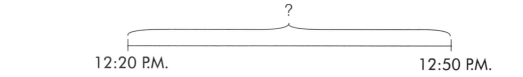

?

12:20 P.M.   12:50 P.M.

Mindy took _____ to travel from the library to her house.

22.

?

7:30 P.M.   8:45 P.M.

Isra's piano lesson lasted _____.

Singapore Math Level 4A & 4B

23.

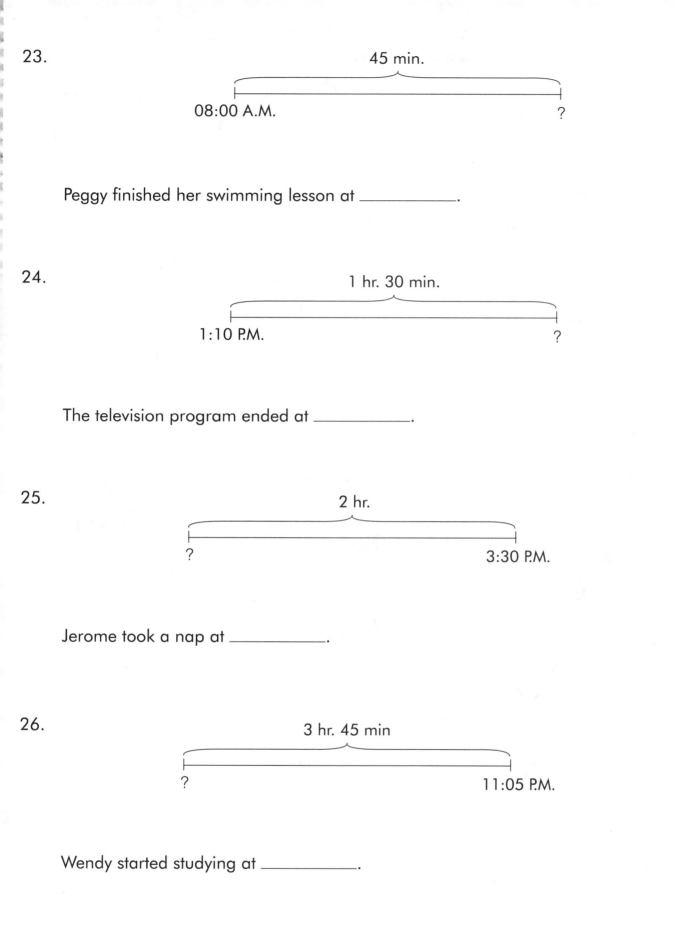

45 min.

08:00 A.M.   ?

Peggy finished her swimming lesson at _____.

24.

1 hr. 30 min.

1:10 P.M.   ?

The television program ended at _____.

25.

2 hr.

?   3:30 P.M.

Jerome took a nap at _____.

26.

3 hr. 45 min

?   11:05 P.M.

Wendy started studying at _____.

Solve the following story problems. Show your work in the space below.

27. Mike started doing his project at 5:15 P.M. He finished his project at 8:30 P.M. How long did he take to do his project?

28. The time shown on Basil's watch is 3:20 P.M. If his watch is 30 minutes fast, what should be the correct time?

Singapore Math Level 4A & 4B

29. Benjamin reached his grandmother's house at 1:40 P.M. If the trip from his house to his grandmother's house took 25 min., at what time did Benjamin leave his house?

30. Mrs. Murray went to a shopping center at 4:00 P.M. She finished her shopping at 5:45 P.M. How long did she spend at the shopping center?

Singapore Math Level 4A & 4B

31. A concert lasted 3 hr. 15 min. If the concert ended at 11:55 P.M., at what time did the concert start?

32. The time it takes for a plane to fly from Boston to Washington, D.C. is 90 min. If the plane leaves Boston at 12:40 P.M., at what time will the plane reach Washington, D.C.?

33. An exam started at 8:05 A.M. It lasted 2 hr. 30 min. At what time did the exam end?

34. A coach traveled from Town X to Town Y. The coach started the trip at 10:35 P.M. and reached Town Y at 7:15 A.M. the next morning. How long was the trip?

35. When it is 9:30 P.M. in New York, the clock in San Francisco shows 12:30 P.M. If the time in San Francisco is 4 P.M., what time is it in New York?

Unit 12: PERIMETER AND AREA

Examples:

1. The area of a rectangular paper is 90 cm². Its length is 10 cm. Find its width.

    Area = Length × Width
    90 cm² = 10 cm × Width
    Width = 90 ÷ 10 = 9 cm

    Its width is **9 cm**.

2. The perimeter of a square is 36 in. Find its area.

    Perimeter = 4 × Length
    36 in. = 4 × Length
    Length = 36 ÷ 4 = 9 in.

    Area = Length × Length
       = 9 × 9
       = 81 in.²

    Its area is **81 in.²**.

3. Find the area of the figure below.

    Area of square = 10 × 10
              = 100 ft.²
    Area of rectangle = 15 × 62
              = 930 ft.²

    100 + 930 = 1,030 ft.²

    The area of the figure is **1,030 ft.²**.

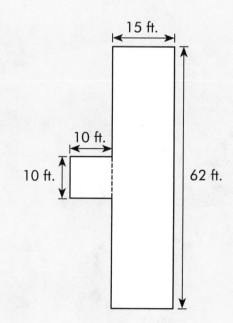

Singapore Math Level 4A & 4B

Find the perimeter and area of each figure.

1.

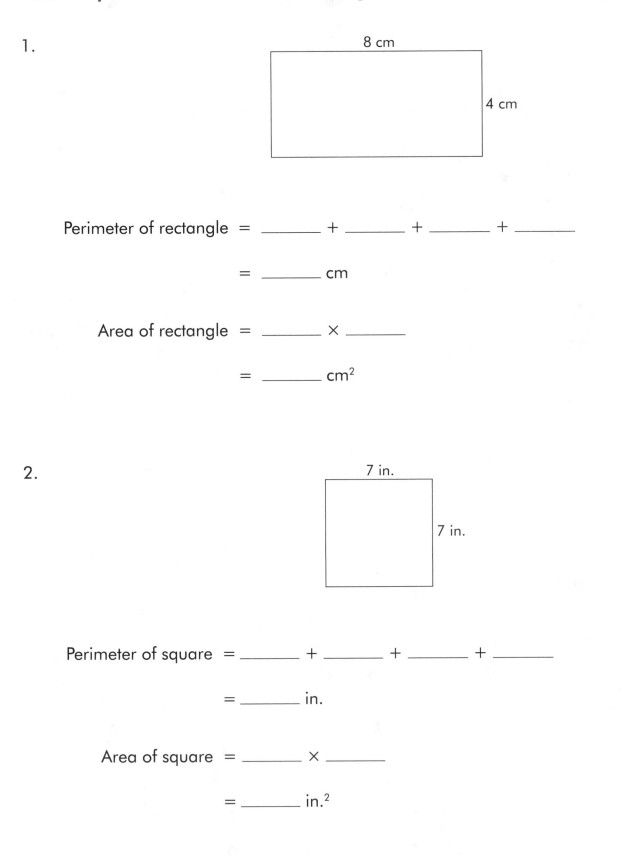

8 cm

4 cm

Perimeter of rectangle = _____ + _____ + _____ + _____

= _____ cm

Area of rectangle = _____ × _____

= _____ cm²

2.

7 in.

7 in.

Perimeter of square = _____ + _____ + _____ + _____

= _____ in.

Area of square = _____ × _____

= _____ in.²

Singapore Math Level 4A & 4B

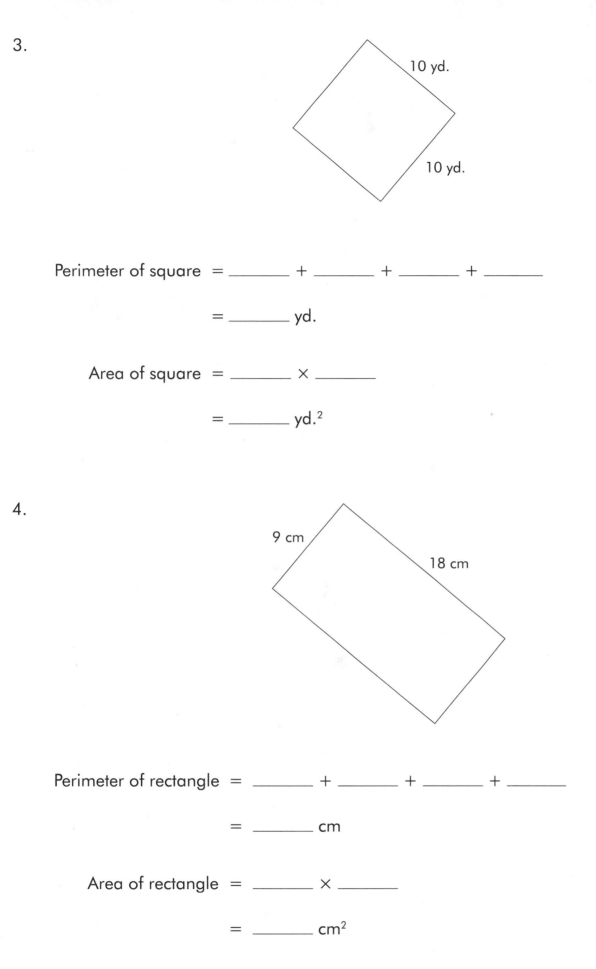

3.

10 yd.

10 yd.

Perimeter of square = _____ + _____ + _____ + _____

= _____ yd.

Area of square = _____ × _____

= _____ yd.^{2}

4.

9 cm

18 cm

Perimeter of rectangle = _____ + _____ + _____ + _____

= _____ cm

Area of rectangle = _____ × _____

= _____ cm^2

5.

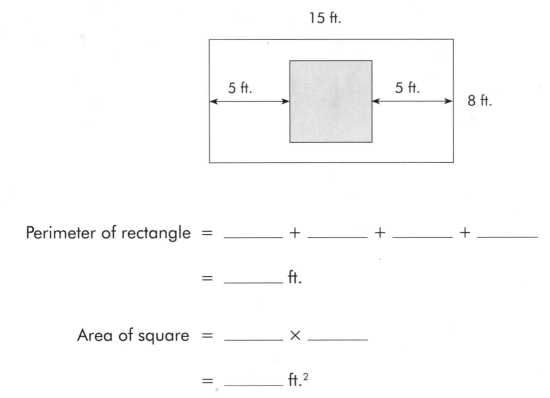

Perimeter of rectangle = _____ + _____ + _____ + _____

= _____ ft.

Area of square = _____ × _____

= _____ ft.^{2}

Solve the problems below. Write your answers on the lines.

6.   The perimeter of a rectangle is 44 in. If the width of the rectangle is 5 in., what is its length?

_____

7.   The perimeter of a square is 52 cm. Find its length.   _____

8.   The area of a rectangle is 36 cm^2. Find the length of the rectangle if its width is 4 cm.

_____

9.   The perimeter of a rectangle is 52 yd. Find its width if its length is 15 yd.

_____

Singapore Math Level 4A & 4B

10. The area of a square is 81 ft.². Find its length. _____

11. The area of a square table is 64 cm². Find the perimeter of the square table.

_____

12. The perimeter of a rectangle is 48 in. If the length of the rectangle is two times its width, what is the area of the rectangle?

_____

13. The perimeter of a table is 6 ft. If the width is 1 ft., find its area.

_____

14. The area of a square room is 16 m². Find the perimeter of the room.

_____

15. The area of a rectangular field is 150 yd.². If its length is $1\frac{1}{2}$ times its width, find the perimeter of the field.

_____

Singapore Math Level 4A & 4B

16. The figure below is made up of two rectangles. Find its perimeter.

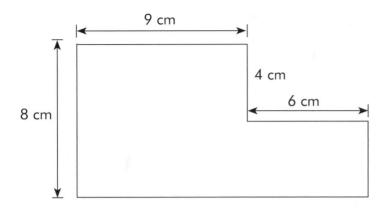

_____

17. The figure below is made up of a square and two rectangles. Find its area.

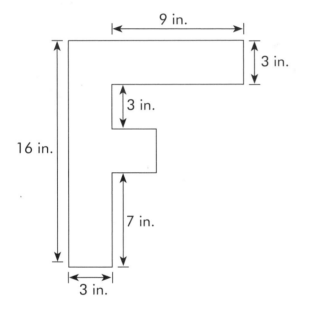

_____

18. The figure below is made up of three rectangles. Find its area and perimeter.

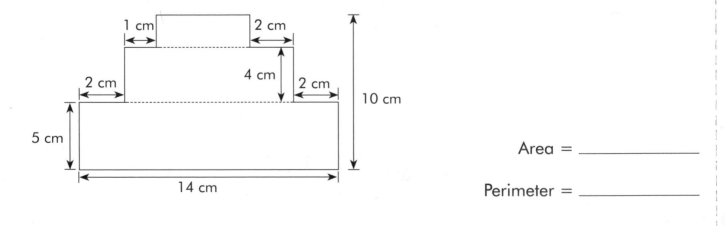

Area = _____

Perimeter = _____

Singapore Math Level 4A & 4B

19. Find the area and perimeter of the figure below.

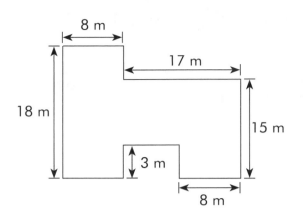

Area = _____

Perimeter = _____

20. Find the area and perimeter of the figure below.

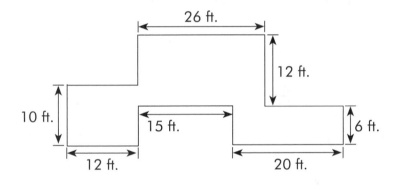

Area = _____

Perimeter = _____

Singapore Math Level 4A & 4B

Solve the following story problems. Show your work in the space below.

21.   The figure below shows the floor plan of Rita's house. How big is her house?

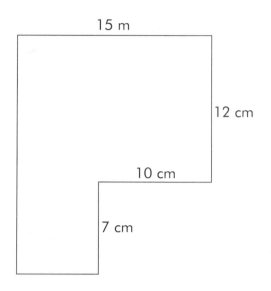

15 m

12 cm

10 cm

7 cm

Singapore Math Level 4A & 4B

22. The figure below shows an exhibition hall. Part of the exhibition hall is covered with carpet. Find the area that is covered with carpet.

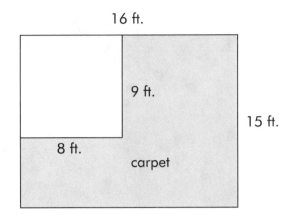

Singapore Math Level 4A & 4B

23. The figure below is made up of six identical squares of a total area of 294 cm². Find the perimeter of the shaded portion.

24. A white rectangular board measuring 28 in. long and 16 in. wide is placed in the center of a larger rectangular board. It creates a border of 3 in. around it. Find the area not covered by the white rectangular board.

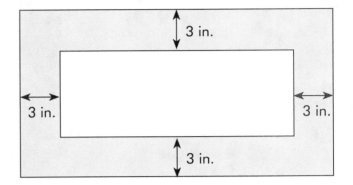

Singapore Math Level 4A & 4B

25. Mary's room measures 8 m by 7 m. If the area not covered by carpet measures 4.5 m by 4 m, find the floor area in her room that is covered by carpet.

26. A farmer had a plot of land measuring 15 yd. by 11 yd. The farmer put up a fence, leaving a margin of 2 yd. wide all round it.

(a) Find the length of the fence.

(b) If the fence cost $3.85 a yard, how much did it cost to put a fence round the plot of land?

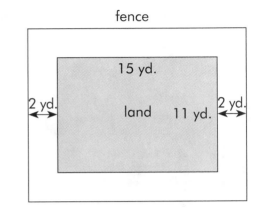

27. Tammy bought a square cardboard. She cut a letter "L" from the cardboard as shown below. Find the remaining area of the cardboard.

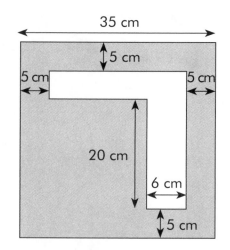

Singapore Math Level 4A & 4B

REVIEW 6

Choose the correct answer. Write its number in the parentheses.

1. The length of a rectangle is 32 in. Its length is twice its width. What is the perimeter of the rectangle?

    (1) 48 in.   (3) 192 in.

    (2) 96 in.   (4) 512 in.   (   )

2. Which of the following shows ten fifty-five and thirty-six seconds at night?

    (1) 10.55.36 P.M.   (3) 1055:36 P.M.

    (2) 10:55:36 P.M.   (4) 10.55:36 P.M.   (   )

3. The length of a square field is 256 m. Paul ran 6 times around the field. Find the total distance that he ran.

    (1) 1,024 m   (3) 4,096 m

    (2) 1,536 m   (4) 6,144 m   (   )

The clocks below show the length of time Brian takes to type a sentence.

4. How many seconds does Brian take to type the sentence?

    (1)   4   (3)   30

    (2)   20   (4)   40   (   )

5. The perimeter of the figure below is _____.

    (1)   36 ft.

    (2)   42 ft.

    (3)   48 ft.

    (4)   51 ft.

    (   )

6. The perimeter of a rectangle is 64 cm. If its length is 19 cm, find its width.

    (1)   13 cm   (3)   22.5 cm

    (2)   15 cm   (4)   26 cm   (   )

7. Jeremy started practicing for his piano recital at 4:40 P.M. He stopped at 6:15 P.M. How long did he practice for his piano recital?

    (1)   1 hr. 45 min.   (3)   1 hr. 25 min.

    (2)   1 hr. 35 min.   (4)   1 hr. 15 min.   (   )

Write your answers on the lines.

8. A square has a perimeter of 40 yd. What is its area?

_____

Singapore Math Level 4A & 4B

9. The figure below is made of 3 rectangles. Find the area of the figure.

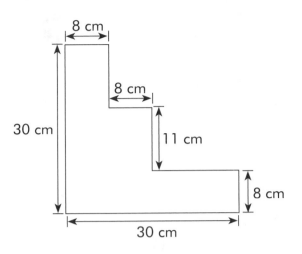

10. The figure is made up of 4 identical squares. It has an area of 256 ft.². What is the length of each square?

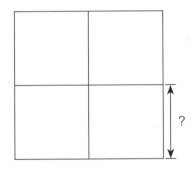

11. The figure below is made up of a square and a rectangle. Square A and Rectangle B have the same area. What is the perimeter of the figure?

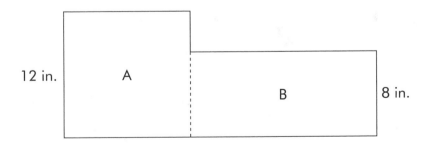

Singapore Math Level 4A & 4B

12. Find the area of the shaded part.

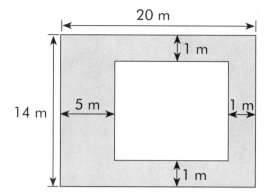

_____

13. Kisha started her school lessons at 7:45 A.M. Her lessons lasted for 5 hr. 30 min. What time did her lessons end?

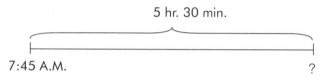

_____

14. Write the time ten twenty-two and forty-three seconds at night.   _____

15. Mandy took 40 sec. to peel an apple. Draw the correct second hand on the clock shown on the right.

Solve the following story problems. Show your work in the space below.

16. Mr. Edmonds wants to tile a 2-foot wide pavement around a swimming pool measuring 15 ft. by 12 ft.

    (a) Find the area of pavement Mr. Edmonds needs to tile.

    (b) How much does he have to pay if the tile costs $29 per square foot?

17. Mr. Simon works from 9:30 P.M. every night. He will stop work at 7:55 A.M. the next day. How long does he work every night?

Singapore Math Level 4A & 4B

18. In the figure, X and Z are identical squares. Y is a bigger square. The area of square X is 49 cm² and the area of square Y is 81 cm². What is the perimeter of the figure?

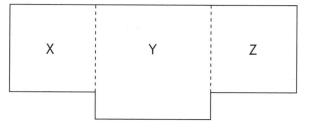

19. Phil has a piece of cardboard of length 120 in. Its width is $\frac{3}{5}$ as long as its length. Find the area of the cardboard.

20. When it is 7:00 A.M. in Denver, the clock in London, England shows 2:00 P.M. If Jennifer wants to call her mother who is in London at 8:00 P.M., at what time should she make the call in Denver?

Singapore Math Level 4A & 4B

Unit 13: SYMMETRY

Examples:

1. Which of the following figures are symmetrical?

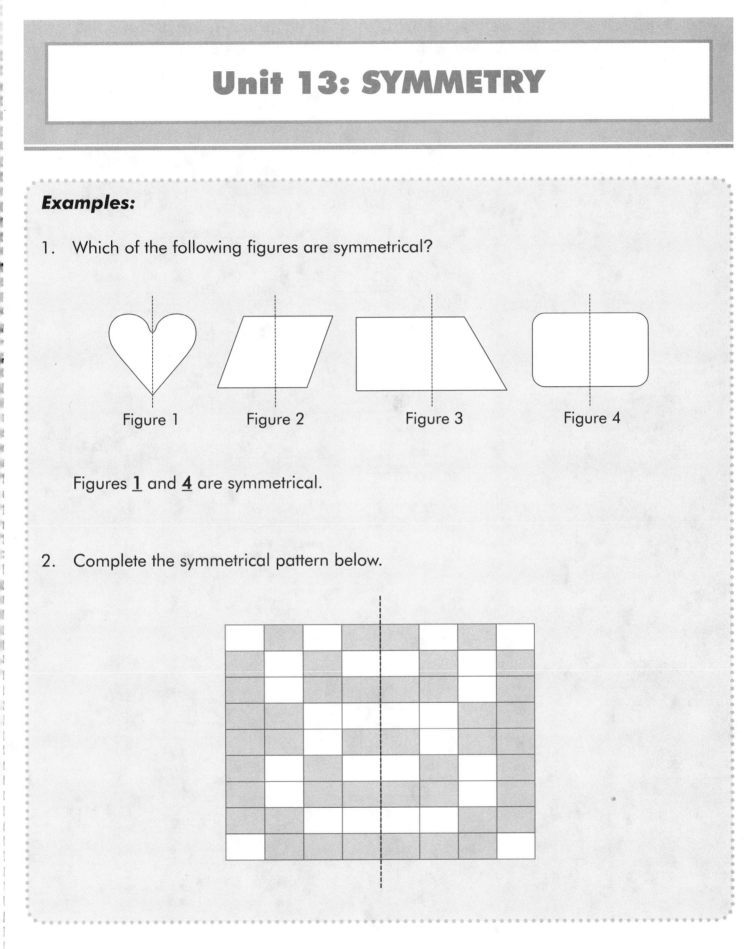

Figure 1   Figure 2   Figure 3   Figure 4

Figures **1** and **4** are symmetrical.

2. Complete the symmetrical pattern below.

Singapore Math Level 4A & 4B

Some of the letters shown below are symmetrical. Write _Yes_ in the blank if the letter is symmetrical and write _No_ in the blank if the letter is not symmetrical.

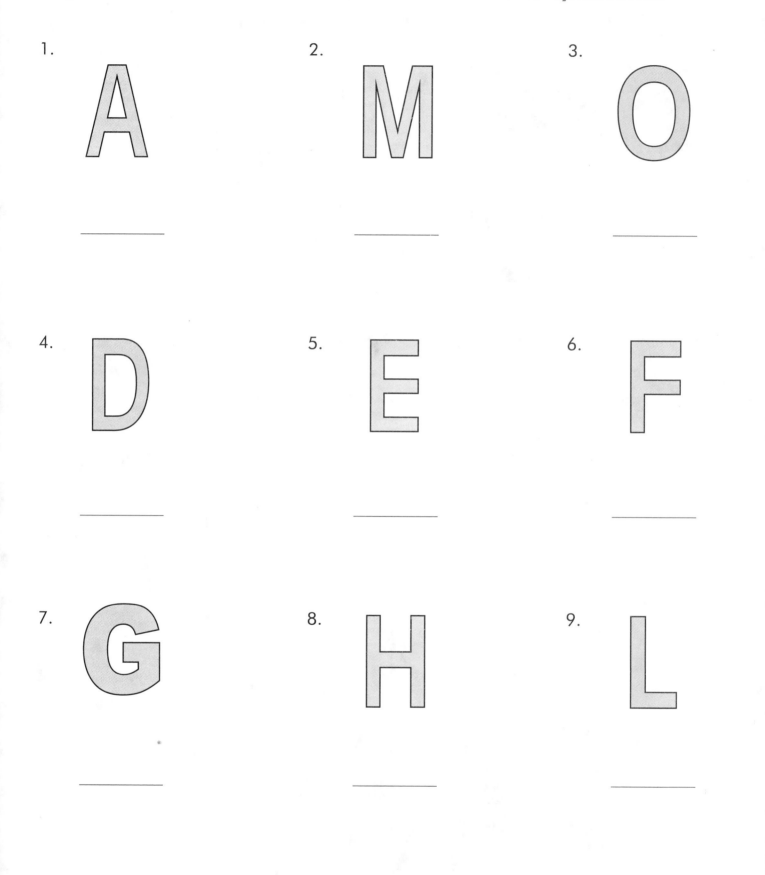

1. A _____

2. M _____

3. O _____

4. D _____

5. E _____

6. F _____

7. G _____

8. H _____

9. L _____

Singapore Math Level 4A & 4B

Study each figure carefully. Write *Yes* **in the blank if the dotted line is a line of symmetry or** *No* **in the blank if the dotted line is not a line of symmetry.**

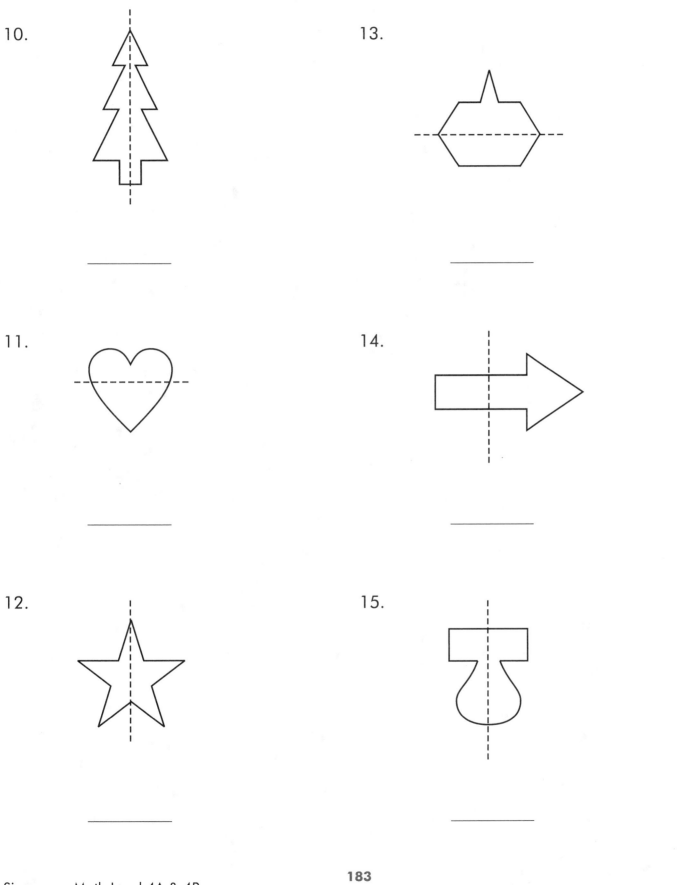

10. _____

11. _____

12. _____

13. _____

14. _____

15. _____

Singapore Math Level 4A & 4B

Complete the symmetrical figures.

16.

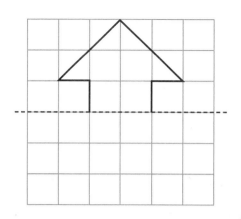

17.

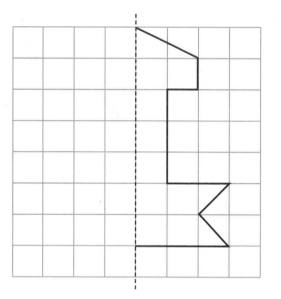

18.

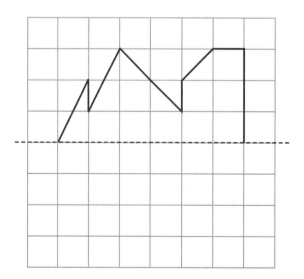

19.

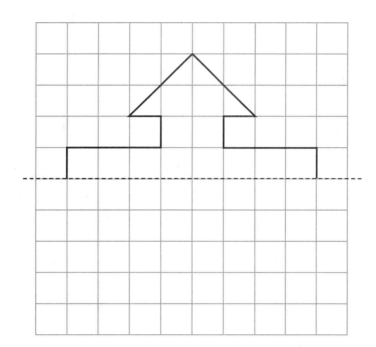

20.

21.

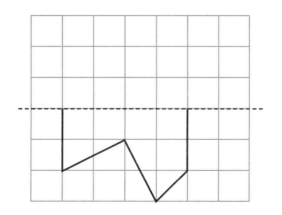

Singapore Math Level 4A & 4B

Complete the symmetrical patterns.

22.

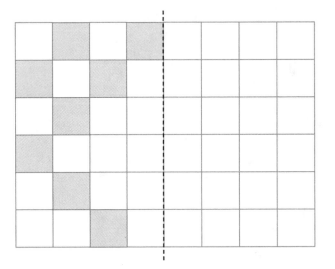

23.

24.

Singapore Math Level 4A & 4B

25.

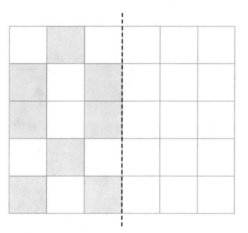

26.

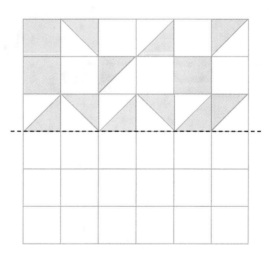

27.

Singapore Math Level 4A & 4B

Unit 14: TESSELLATIONS

Examples:

1. Identify the unit shape in the tessellation below.

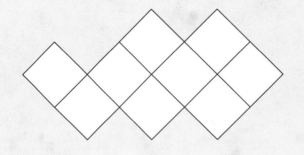

    The unit shape is ◇.

2. Make a tessellation of the unit shape by adding 8 more unit shapes.

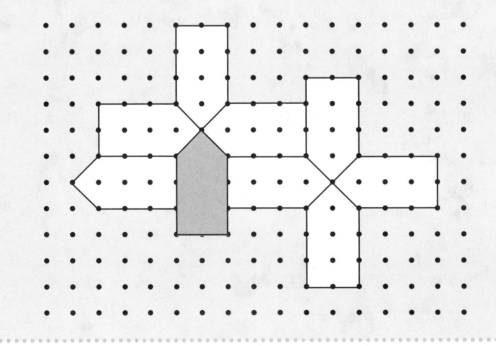

Singapore Math Level 4A & 4B

For each tessellation, identify the unit shape by shading it.

1.

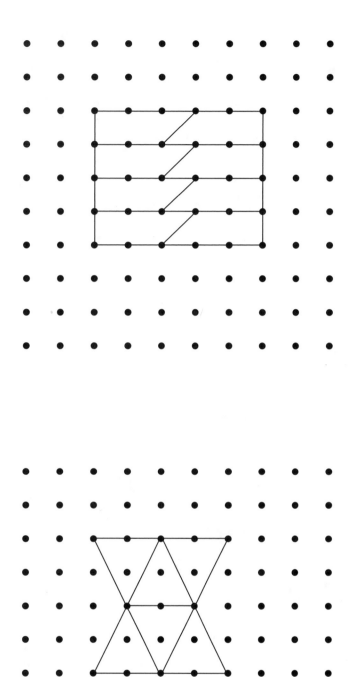

2.

Singapore Math Level 4A & 4B

3.

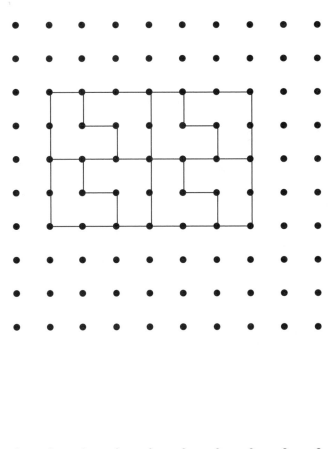

4.

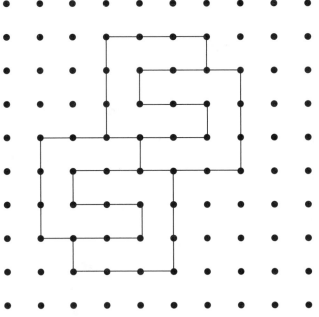

Singapore Math Level 4A & 4B

5.

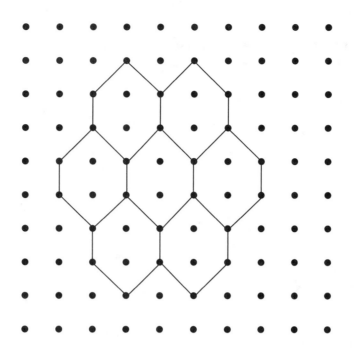

State if the following shapes tessellate or repeat without gaps or overlaps. Write Yes in the blank if it tessellates or No if it does not tessellate.

6.

Singapore Math Level 4A & 4B

7.

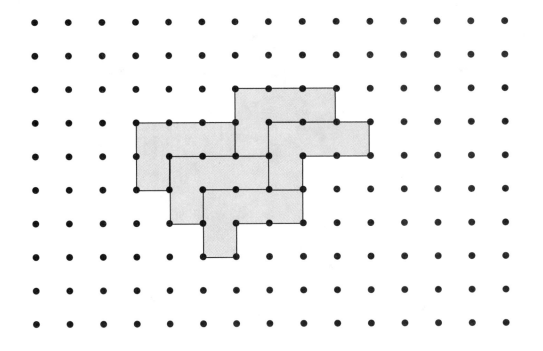

8.

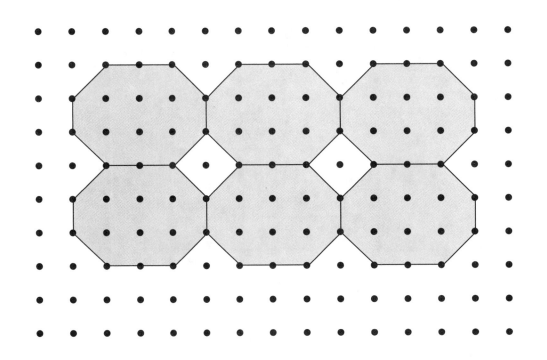

Singapore Math Level 4A & 4B

9.

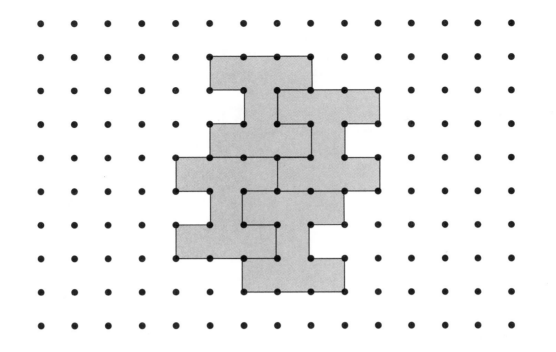

_____

10.

_____

Singapore Math Level 4A & 4B

Complete each tessellation by adding 5 more unit shapes to it.

11.

12.

Singapore Math Level 4A & 4B

13.

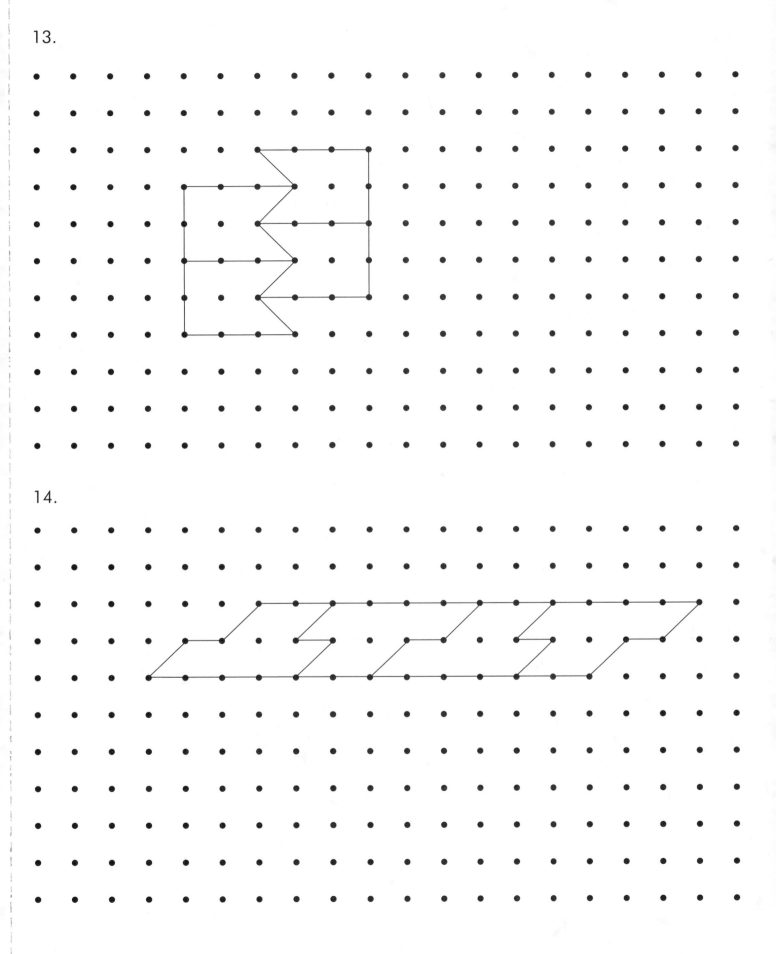

14.

Singapore Math Level 4A & 4B

15.

Draw the following shapes in 2 different tessellations. Add at least 5 more unit shapes.

16. (a)

(b)

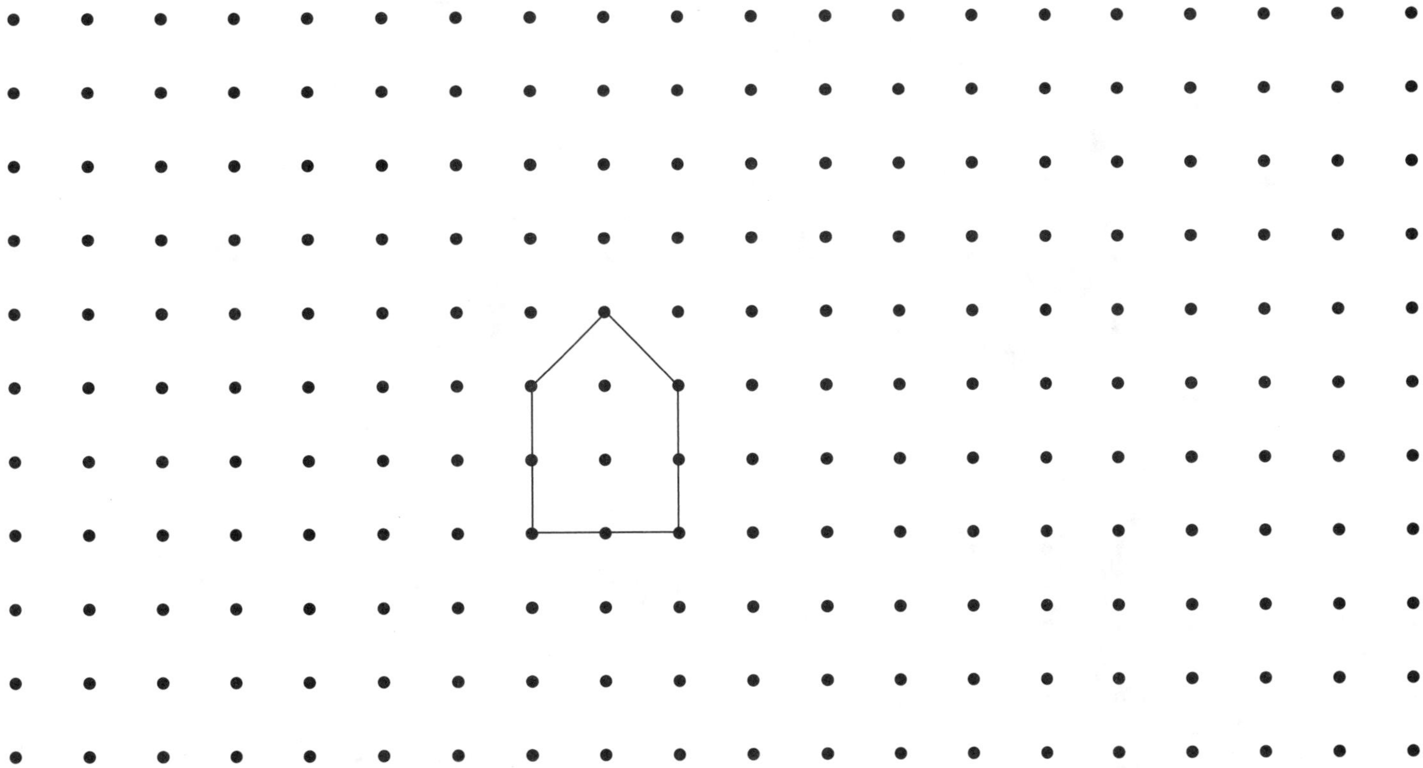

17. (a)

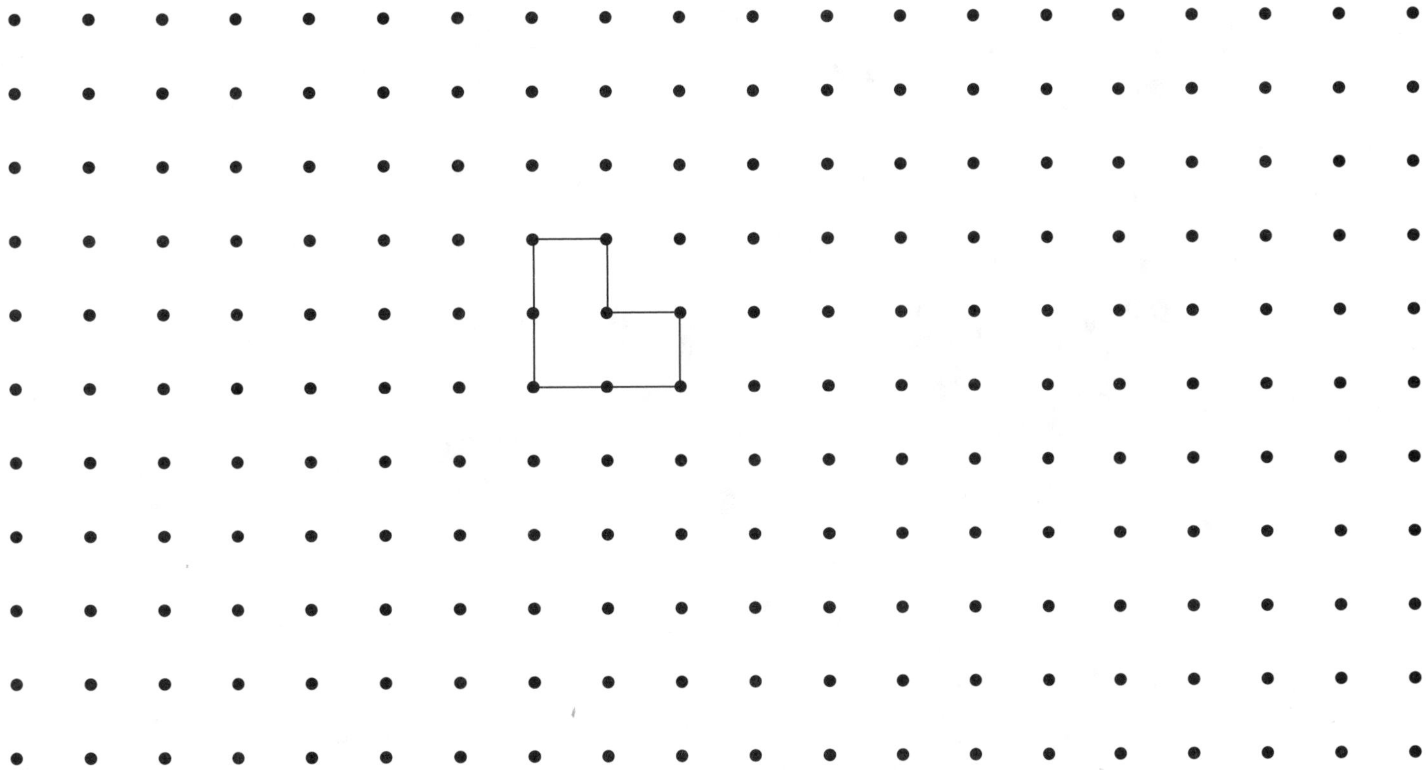

Singapore Math Level 4A & 4B

(b)

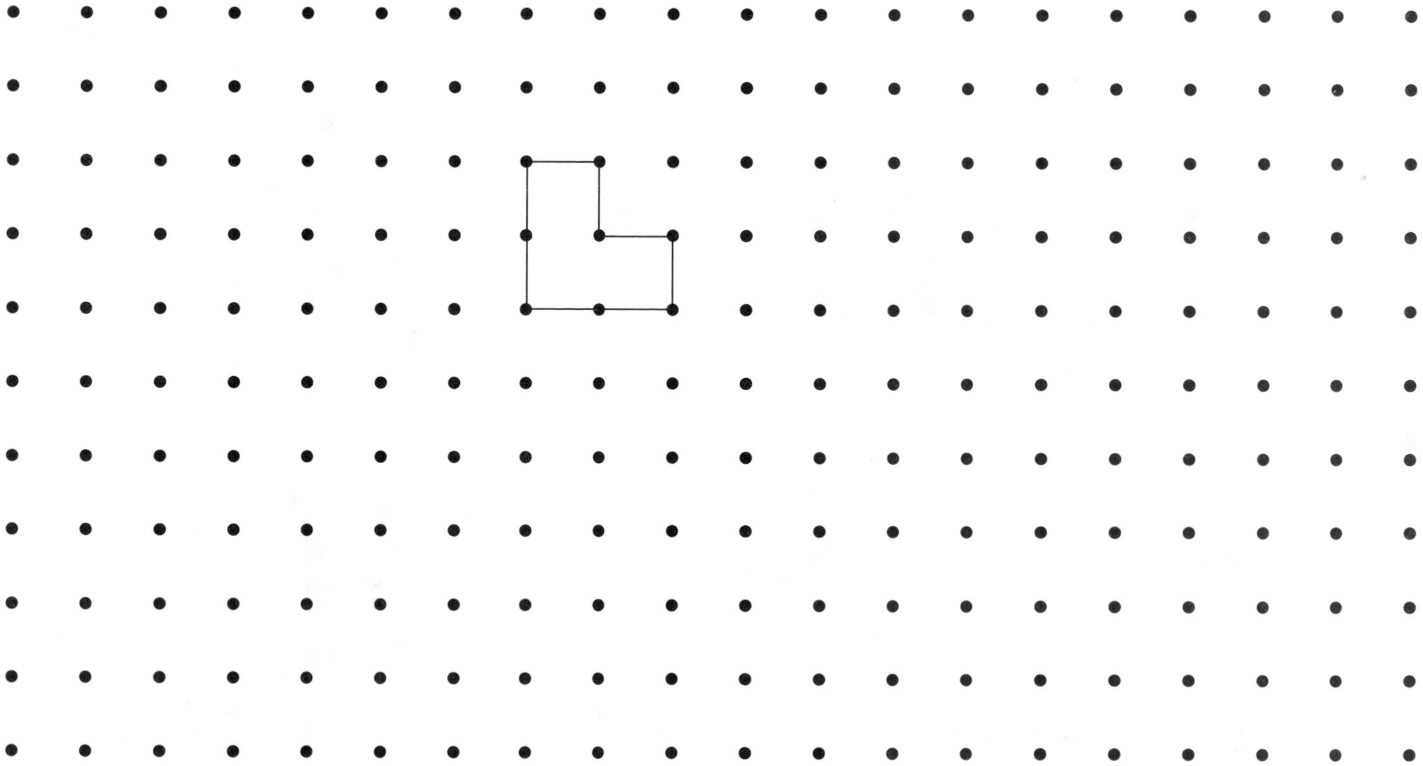

REVIEW 7

Choose the correct answer. Write its number in the parentheses.

1. Which of the following figures is symmetrical?

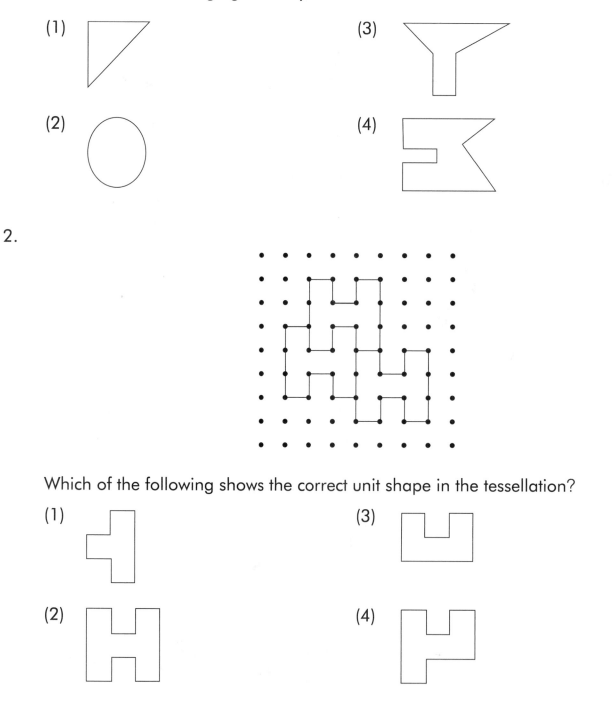

(1)

(2)

(3)

(4)

(   )

2.

Which of the following shows the correct unit shape in the tessellation?

(1)

(2)

(3)

(4)

(   )

3. Which of the following figures are symmetrical?

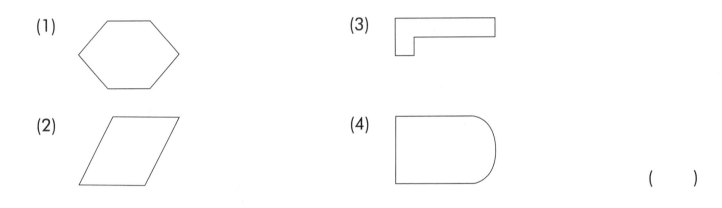

A   B   C   D   E

(1)   A and C   (3)   B and C
(2)   A and D   (4)   B and E   (   )

4. Which of the following shapes cannot be tessellated?

(1)   (3)

(2)   (4)

(   )

5. How many more squares must be shaded to make the figure below symmetrical? (2 right-angled triangles make up 1 square.)

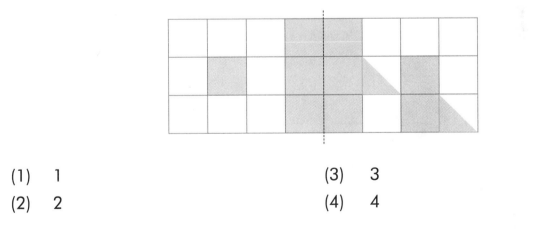

(1)   1   (3)   3
(2)   2   (4)   4   (   )

Singapore Math Level 4A & 4B

6. Which of the following shows the correct line of symmetry?

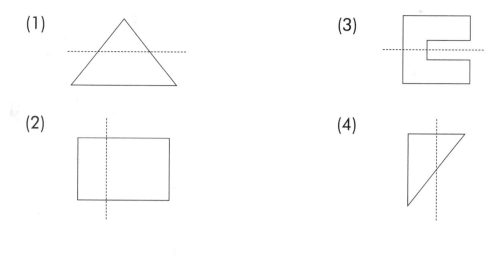

(1)

(3)

(2)

(4)

(   )

7. Which of the following shapes can be tessellated?

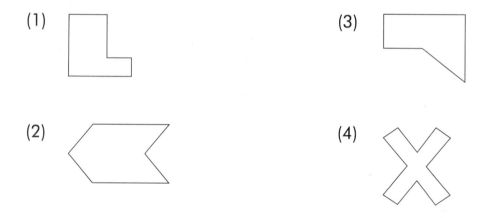

(1)

(3)

(2)

(4)

(   )

Write your answers on the lines.

8. State if the dotted line is a line of symmetry.

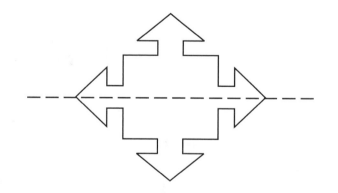

_____

Singapore Math Level 4A & 4B

9. The figure below shows half of a symmetrical figure. Line XY is the line of symmetry. Complete the other half of the symmetrical figure.

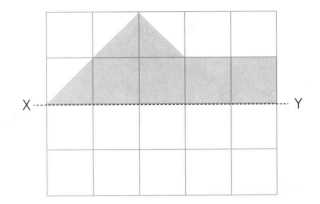

10. Complete the tessellation by adding 5 more unit shapes to it.

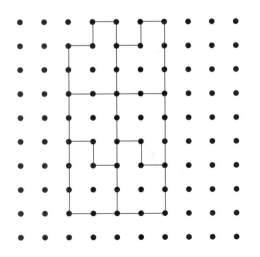

11. Identify the unit shape in the tessellation below by shading it.

Singapore Math Level 4A & 4B

12. Is the figure below symmetrical?

_____

13. Complete the symmetrical figure.

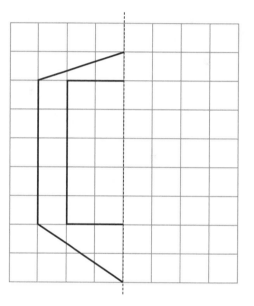

14. Complete the tessellation by adding 5 more unit shapes to it.

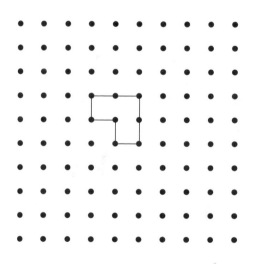

Singapore Math Level 4A & 4B

15. Complete the symmetrical figure.

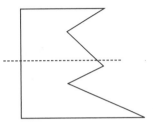

16. State if the dotted line is a line of symmetry.

_____

17. Identify the unit shape in the tessellation below by shading it.

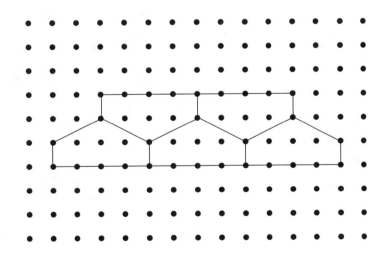

Singapore Math Level 4A & 4B

18. Complete the symmetrical figure.

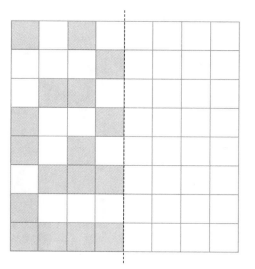

19. State if the letter 'Z' below is symmetrical.

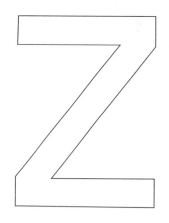

_____

Singapore Math Level 4A & 4B

Draw the following shape in 2 different tessellations. Add at least 5 more unit shapes.

20.

Singapore Math Level 4A & 4B

208

Choose the correct answer. Write its number in the parentheses.

1. The sum of 28.16 and 5.09 is _____.

   (1) 32.25   (3) 33.25

   (2) 33.16   (4) 34.06   (   )

2. The length of a rope is 5 m when rounded to the nearest meter. Which of the following is the original length of the rope?

   (1) 4 m 40 cm   (3) 5 m 50 cm

   (2) 4 m 60 cm   (4) 5 m 60 cm   (   )

3. Johnny looked at the clock when he was washing his hands. The second hand moved from 3 to 8. He then stopped washing his hands. How long did he wash his hands?

   (1) 5 sec.   (3) 25 sec.

   (2) 15 sec.   (4) 35 sec.   (   )

4. Which of the following numbers is symmetrical?

   (1) 3   (3) 5

   (2) 4   (4) 6   (   )

5. $8.604 = 8 + 0.6 +$ _____

   (1) 4   (3) 0.04

   (2) 0.4   (4) 0.004   (   )

6. Write the time one seventeen and forty-two seconds in the morning.

   (1) 0117:42   (3) 1.17:42 A.M.

   (2) 1:17:42 A.M.   (4) 01:17.42   (   )

Singapore Math Level 4A & 4B

7. Write 4 tens, 15 tenths, and 3 hundredths in numerals.

   (1)   4.153   (3)   40.18

   (2)   40.153   (4)   41.53   (   )

8. $21.04 = 21 + \dfrac{4}{\Box}$. What should be the correct answer in the box?

   (1)   1   (3)   100

   (2)   10   (4)   1000   (   )

9. The perimeter of a square is 64 in. Find its length.

   (1)   8 in.   (3)   18 in.

   (2)   16 in.   (4)   32 in.   (   )

10. Express 405 hundredths as a decimal.

   (1)   0.405   (3)   40.5

   (2)   4.05   (4)   400.5   (   )

11. The product of 93.28 and 8 is _____.

   (1)   11.66   (3)   101.28

   (2)   85.28   (4)   746.24   (   )

12. Which of the following figures below is **not** symmetrical?

   (1)   (3)

   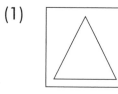

   (2)   (4)

                                                                    (   )

13. Fiona watched a cartoon at 7:30 P.M. If the cartoon ended at 9:10 P.M., how long was the cartoon?

    (1) 1 hr. 20 min.   (3) 2 hr. 10 min.

    (2) 1 hr. 40 min.   (4) 2 hr. 20 min.   (   )

14. Lisa bought 5.4 kg of sugar. She packed the sugar equally into 4 bags. What was the mass of each bag of sugar?

    (1) 1.26 kg   (3) 9.4 kg

    (2) 1.35 kg   (4) 21.6 kg   (   )

15. Mrs. Volkmer sold 100 cookies. She sold them at $2.05 for 10 cookies. How much money did she collect from selling the cookies?

    (1) $20.50   (3) $200.50

    (2) $25   (4) $205   (   )

16. Ben took 18.35 sec. to complete a 100-yard race. Daniel finished the race 3.2 sec. faster than Ben. How long did Daniel take to finish the race?

    (1) 15.15 sec.   (3) 18.07 sec.

    (2) 15.33 sec.   (4) 21.55 sec.   (   )

17. The perimeter of a square is 20 ft. Find its area.

    (1) 16 ft.^{2} (3) 80 ft.^{2}

    (2) 25 ft.^{2} (4) 400 ft.^{2} (   )

18. The figure, not drawn to scale, is made up of 5 similar squares. Find its perimeter.

    (1) 16 cm
    (2) 32 cm
    (3) 48 cm
    (4) 80 cm

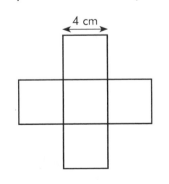

4 cm

                                                                              (   )

Singapore Math Level 4A & 4B

19. Which of the following decimals is 10 when rounding to the nearest whole number?

   (1) 9.09   (3) 10.5

   (2) 9.9   (4) 10.9   (   )

20. In 805.139, which digit is in the thousandths place?

   (1) 3   (3) 8

   (2) 5   (4) 9   (   )

Write your answers on the lines.

21. The shaded parts represent the decimal. Write down the correct decimal.

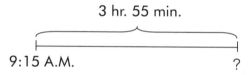

   _____

22. Tomas reached the library at 9:15 A.M. He stayed there for 3 hr. 55 min. At what time did he leave the library?

   3 hr. 55 min.

   9:15 A.M.   ?

   _____

23. Express $\frac{4}{5}$ as a decimal.   _____

24. Shade 0.25 of the figure below.

Singapore Math Level 4A & 4B

25. State if the shape below is symmetrical.

_____

26. Identify the unit shape in the tessellation below by shading it.

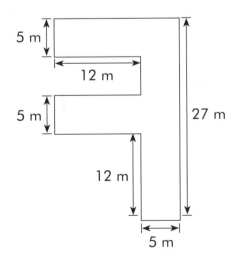

27. Arrange the decimals in descending order.

7.8   0.78   7.08

_____

28. The figure below is made up of three rectangles. Find its area.

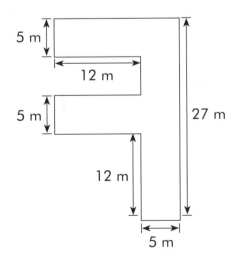

Singapore Math Level 4A & 4B

29. Complete the symmetrical figure.

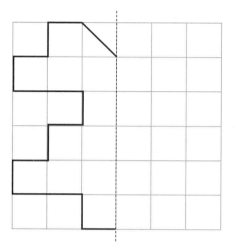

30. Estimate the value of 41.8 ÷ 6.

_____

31. A clock shows 4:40 P.M. If the clock is 45 minutes slow, write the correct time.

_____

32. The figure is made up of 5 squares. Find its area.

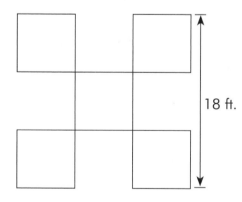

18 ft.

_____

Singapore Math Level 4A & 4B

33. Complete the symmetrical pattern below using Line AB as the line of symmetry.

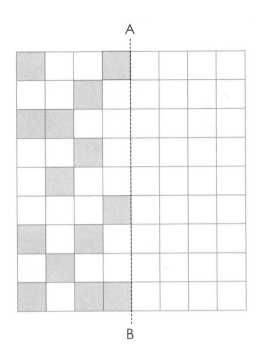

34. Rudy poured 9 gallons of syrup into 5 bottles equally. How much syrup was there in each bottle?

_____

35. Complete the tessellation below by adding 5 more unit shapes.

Singapore Math Level 4A & 4B

36. A garden has an area of 96 yd.². Its width is 6 yd. Find its perimeter.

_____

37. In 127.04, the digit 0 is in the [ ] place.

_____

38. Fill in each box with the correct decimal.

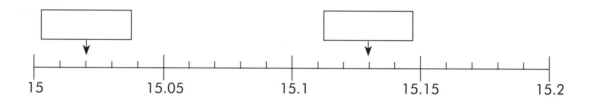

39.

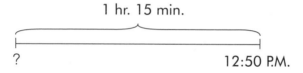

Cara got off the bus at 12:50 P.M. If the trip took 1 hr. 15 min., at what time did she board the bus?

_____

40. State if the unit shape below can be tessellated.

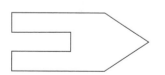

_____

Solve the following story problems. Show your work in the space below.

41. Mrs. Brown bought 13 lb. of meat. Each pound of meat cost $9.65. She gave the cashier $150. How much change did she receive?

42. A bus left Townsville at 7:05 P.M. It traveled for 3 hr. 40 min. and stopped for a rest. The bus continued the journey and reached Garden Town at 3:30 A.M. If the second part of the journey was 4 hr. 10 min., how long did it stop for a rest?

Singapore Math Level 4A & 4B

43. To make a bottle of fruit punch, 0.84 L of orange juice, 0.47 L of ginger ale, and 0.65 L of pineapple juice are needed. How many liters of fruit punch are there in a dozen bottles?

44. Charlene used 1.6 m of ribbon to tie a large present. She used another 95 cm of ribbon to tie a small present. If she had 5 m of ribbon in the beginning, how many meters of ribbon did she have left?

45. A carpet is placed in the middle of a square hall as shown below. What is the total cost of the carpet if it costs $19 per yd.²?

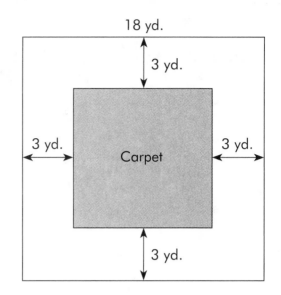

CHALLENGE QUESTIONS

Solve the following problems on another sheet of paper.

1. Study the pattern carefully and draw the correct shape in the given box.

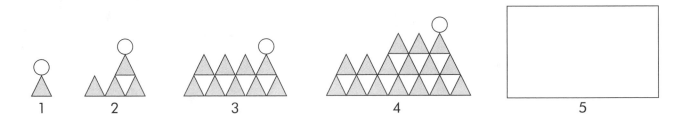

2. A group of students were told that they would have their afternoon break when the hour hand and minute hand formed a right angle on the clock. If the minute hand pointed to 12, what was the time of their afternoon break?

3. Two similar television sets and one DVD player cost $919.70.
   One television set and two similar DVD players cost $639.70.
   How much do three television sets cost?

4. The area of the bigger square is 576 in.². The area of the shaded square is 144 in.². Find the length of x.

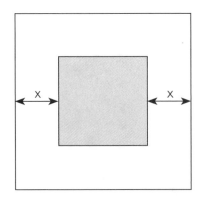

5. Several 3-cm cubes are arranged to form a solid as shown below. Find the total perimeter of all the faces of the solid.

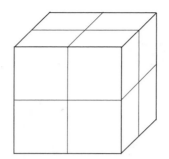

6. Mrs. Munoz sold three times as much lemon tea on Saturday than on Monday. She sold 5 times as much lemon tea on Sunday than on Monday. If Mrs. Munoz sold 2 liters 600 milliliters more of lemon tea on Sunday than on Saturday, how much lemon tea did Mrs. Munoz sell over the weekend?

7. How many 1-in. cubes are needed to make this 3-in. solid?

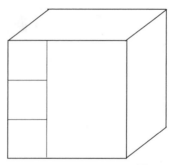

8. Three similar books and two similar dictionaries cost $85.50.
One book and one dictionary cost $37.80.
How much is each book?

Singapore Math Level 4A & 4B

9. The length of the bigger square is 64 cm. Find the area of the unshaded square.

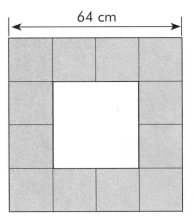

64 cm

10. Circle the letter(s) that is/are **not** symmetrical.

11. How many 5-cm cubes are needed to form a solid of 3,125 cm³?

12. Keith took an hour to paint 5 similar chairs. If he worked 8 hours a day, how many days did he use to paint 120 similar chairs?

Singapore Math Level 4A & 4B

SOLUTIONS
Singapore Math Level 4A

Unit 1: Whole Numbers (Part 1)

1. twenty-three thousand, seven hundred, one
2. forty thousand, eight hundred, twenty-five
3. sixty-eight thousand, ninety
4. fifty-five thousand, two
5. fourteen thousand, eleven
6. **11,602**
7. **92,314**
8. **57,012**
9. **60,245**
10. **82,001**
11. **6, 20, 300, 5,000, 10,000**
12. **7, 10, 200, 8,000, 50,000**
13. **5, 30, 0, 8,000, 70,000**
14. **0, 20, 400, 1,000, 80,000**
15. **ten thousands**
16. **tens**
17. **8**
18. **0**
19. (a) **80,000/80 thousands**
    (b) **1,000/1 thousand**
    (c) **200/2 hundreds**
    (d) **40/4 tens**
    (e) **6/6 ones**
20. **2**
21. **1**
22. **3**
23. **6**
24. **3,000**
25. **10**
26. **9,000**
27. **100**
28. **80,000**
29. **49,561**
30. **98,075**
31. **13,689**
32. **9,173**
33. **1,359, 1,593, 5,319, 5,931**
34. **12,643, 14,632, 24,163, 41,562**
35. **4,586, 4,685, 6,845, 8,564**
36. **7,410, 7,014, 1,740, 1,407**
37. **96,268, 63,892, 39,628, 26,983**
38. **5,362, 5,236, 3,652, 2,653**
39. **286, 306**
    246 – 126 = 20
    20 + 266 = 286
    20 + 286 = 306
40. **33,055, 33,060**
    33,050 – 33,045 = 5
    5 + 33,050 = 33,055
    5 + 33,055 = 33,060

41. **7,530, 7,560**
    7,550 – 7,540 = 10
    7,540 – 10 = 7,530
    7,550 + 10 = 7,560
42. **90,455, 91,455**
    89,455 – 88,455 = 1,000
    1,000 + 89,455 = 90,455
    1,000 + 90,455 = 91,455
43. **43,012**
    43,112 – 100 = 43,012
44. **94,586**
    94,606 – 20 = 94,586
45. **20,096**
    18,096 + 2,000 = 20,096
46. **81,493**
    80,493 + 1,000 = 81,493
47. **18,475**
    21,475 – 3,000 = 18,475
48. **9,900**
    10,000 – 100 = 9,900
49. **10,381**
    6,000 + 4,381 = 10,381
50. **90,099**
    99 + 90,000 = 90,099

Unit 2: Whole Numbers (Part 2)

1. **770**
2. **850**
3. **660**
4. **300**
5. **1,090**
6. **1,780**
7. **39,920**
8. **46,550**
9. **11,200**
10. **60,000**
11. **500**
12. **900**
13. **3,100**
14. **1,100**
15. **6,900**
16. **89,500**
17. **23,900**
18. **12,100**
19. **61,300**
20. **74,800**
21. **40 + 10 = 50**
22. **670 + 50 = 720**
23. **70 + 730 = 800**
24. **930 – 20 = 910**

25. **420 − 40 = 380**
26. **520 − 20 = 500**
27. **50 × 8 = 400**
28. **30 × 7 = 210**
29. **300 − 10 = 290**
30. **700 − 90 = 610**
31. **120 ÷ 4 = 30**
32. **320 ÷ 5 = 64**
33. **460 + 90 + 550 = 1,100**
34. **880 + 120 + 40 = 1,040**
35. **1, 12**
    2, 6
    3, 4
    1, 2, 3, 4, 6, 12
36. **1, 42**
    2, 21
    3, 14
    6, 7
    1, 2, 3, 6, 7, 14, 21, 42
37. **1, 36**
    2, 18
    3, 12
    4, 9
    6, 6
    1, 2, 3, 4, 6, 9, 12, 18, 36
38. (a) **1, 2, 4, 8**
    (b) **1, 2, 4, 8, 16**
    (c) **1, 2, 4, 8**
39. (a) **1, 2, 7, 14**
    (b) **1, 2, 4, 7, 14, 28**
    (c) **1, 2, 7, 14**
40. (a) **1, 3, 9**
    (b) **1, 2, 3, 6, 9, 18**
    (c) **1, 3, 9**
41. **5, 10, 15, 20**
42. **9, 18, 27**
43. **18**
44. **35**
45. (a) **2, 4, 6, 8, 10, 12**
    (b) **3, 6, 9, 12, 15, 18**
    (c) **6, 12**
46. (a) **4, 8, 12, 16, 20, 24**
    (b) **8, 16, 24, 32, 40, 48**
    (c) **8, 16, 24**
47. 13,800 + 25,300 = **39,100 km**
48. 25,000 − 7,982 = 17,018
    17,018 ≈ **17,020**
49. 1,345 + 7,609 = 8,954
    8,954 ≈ **8,960 books**
50. 1,124 + 259 = 1,383
    1,124 + 1,383 = 2,507
    2,507 ≈ **2,500 students**
51. **10**
    The factors of 10 are 1, 2, 5, and 10.
52. **56**
    56 = 8 × 7
53. **24**
    8 × 3 = 24
    48 = 2 × 24

54. **8**
    32 = 4 × 8
55. **2** and **7**
    2 × 7 = 14
    2 × 14 = 28
    7 × 4 = 28
    The multiples of 2 are 2, 4, 6, 8, 10, 12, ⑭, 16, 18, 20, 22, 24, 26, ㉘, 30, ...
    The multiples of 7 are 7, ⑭, 21, ㉘, 35, ...
    The 2 one-digit numbers are 2 and 7.

Review 1

1. **(1)**
   72,845 is seventy-two thousand, eight hundred, forty-five.
2. **(2)**
   The digit 8 stands for 8,000/8 thousands.
3. **(1)**
   18 ÷ 8 = 2 R 2   18 ÷ 6 = 3
   24 ÷ 8 = 3   24 ÷ 6 = 4
   72 ÷ 8 = 9   72 ÷ 6 = 12
   144 ÷ 8 = 18   144 ÷ 6 = 24
   Therefore 18 is not a common multiple of 8 and 6.
4. **(3)**
   1,987 + 5,248 ≈ 1,990 + 5,250 = 7,240
5. **(2)**
   Factors of 28: 1, 2, 4, 7, 14, 28
   Factors of 36: 1, 2, 3, 4, 6, 9, 12, 18, 36
   The common factors of 28 and 36 are 1, 2, and 4.
6. **(3)**
   7,030 − 6,020 = 1,010
   9,050 − 1,010 = 8,040
7. **(1)**
   10,000 − 2,000 = 8,000
   8,000 − 2,000 = 6,000
   2,000 + 1,000 = 3,000
   2,000 + 800 = 2,800
8. **(2)**
   The first four multiples of 7 are 7, 14, 21, and 28.
9. **(3)**
   49,753 = 40,000 + 9,000 + 700 + 50 + 3
   40,000 is 4 ten thousands.
10. **(1)**
    400 × 9 = 3,600
11. **forty-nine thousand, five**
12. **thousands**
13. **15,005, 15,050, 15,500**
14. **1,520**
    559 + 19 + 942 ≈ 560 + 20 + 940 = 1,520
15. **63**
    7 × 9 = 63
16. **89,100**
17. **50,907**
    50,000 + 900 + 7 = 50,907
18. **1, 3, 5, 9, 15, 45**
    1 × 45 = 45
    3 × 15 = 45
    5 × 9 = 45

Singapore Math Level 4A & 4B

The factors of 45 are 1, 3, 5, 9, 15, and 45.

19. **0**
18,360 + 2,598 = 20,958

20. **12** and **24**
Multiples of 4: 4, 8, ⑫, 16, 20, ㉔, 28, ...
Multiples of 6: 6, ⑫, 18, ㉔, 30, 36, 42, 48, ...

Unit 3: Whole Numbers (Part 3)

1.
```
    4 1 2
  ×     4
  1,6 4 8
```

2.
```
      ¹
    5 4 7
  ×     2
  1,0 9 4
```

3.
```
    6 1 0
  ×     5
  3,0 5 0
```

4.
```
    ¹ ¹
    9 3 5
  ×     3
  2,8 0 5
```

5.
```
      ⁶
    1 0 9
  ×     7
    7 6 3
```

6.
```
  ¹ ¹ ⁴
  5,3 1 7
  ×      6
  3 1,9 0 2
```

7.
```
    2,0 1 1
  ×       8
  1 6,0 8 8
```

8.
```
  ² ⁷
  6,0 2 8
  ×      9
  5 4,2 5 2
```

9.
```
  ² ¹ ³
  1,5 2 6
  ×      5
  7,6 3 0
```

10.
```
  ³ ² ⁵
  8,4 3 7
  ×      8
  6 7,4 9 6
```

11.
```
      ⁴
      4 6
  ×   1 8
    3 6 8
    4 6
    8 2 8
```

12.
```
      ¹
      3 5
  ×   2 0
      0 0
    7 0
    7 0 0
```

13.
```
    ² 
    ⁴
    6 7
  ×   3 6
    4 0 2
  2 0 1
  2,4 1 2
```

14.
```
      9 1
  ×   2 7
    6 3 7
  1,8 2
  2,4 5 7
```

15.
```
      ⁵
      8 9
  ×   1 6
    5 3 4
    8 9
  1,4 2 4
```

16.
```
    ¹ ³
    1 2 6
  ×    5 0
    0 0 0
    6 3 0
  6,3 0 0
```

17.
```
    ¹ ³
    ⁵
    6 2 5
  ×    7 3
    1 8 7 5
  4 3 7 5
  4 5,6 2 5
```

18.
```
    ¹ ³
    6 1 9
  ×    2 4
    2 4 7 6
  1 2 3 8
  1 4,8 5 6
```

19.
```
    ⁴
    ²
    2 8 1
  ×    5 3
    8 4 3
  1 4 0 5
  1 4,8 9 3
```

20.
```
    ²
    ⁴
    3 8 0
  ×    3 6
    2 2 8 0
  1 1 4 0
  1 3,6 8 0
```

21.
```
        2 7 1
  5 ) 1,3 5 5
        1 0
        3 5
        3 5
            5
            5
            0
```

22.
```
      1 6 0 9
  3 ) 4,8 2 7
      3
      1 8
      1 8
          2 0
          0
          2 7
          2 7
          0
```

226

Singapore Math Level 4A & 4B

23.
```
      4, 9 0 2
  2 ) 9, 8 0 4
      8
      1 8
      1 8
          0
          0
            4
            4
            0
```

24.
```
        7 6 1
  8 ) 6, 0 8 8
      5 6
        4 8
        4 8
            8
            8
            0
```

25.
```
        2 4 3
  6 ) 1, 4 5 8
      1 2
        2 5
        2 4
            1 8
            1 8
              0
```

26.
```
        3 7 7
  3 ) 1, 1 3 1
      9
      2 3
      2 1
          2 1
          2 1
            0
```

27. 18, 2, 36, 360
28. 69, 4, 276, 2,760
29. 98, 3, 294, 2,940
30. 53, 6, 318, 3,180
31. 77, 9, 693, 6,930
32. 42, 8, 336, 3,360
33 571, 1
```
          5 7 1
  8 ) 4, 5 6 9
      4 0
        5 6
        5 6
            9
            8
            1
```

34. 269, 3
```
          2 6 9
  5 ) 1, 3 4 8
      1 0
        3 4
        3 0
            4 8
            4 5
              3
```

35. 605, 5
```
          6 0 5
  7 ) 4, 2 4 0
      4 2
          4
          0
          4 0
          3 5
            5
```

36. 783, 2
```
          7 8 3
  4 ) 3, 1 3 4
      2 8
        3 3
        3 2
          1 4
          1 2
            2
```

37. 1042, 3
```
        1, 0 4 2
  9 ) 9, 3 8 1
      9
        3
        0
        3 8
        3 6
          2 1
          1 8
            3
```

38. 60, 20, 1,200
39. 600, 60, 36,000
40. 900, 30, 27,000
41. 240, 48
42. 4,900, 700
43. 8,100, 900

44. (a) 4,368
    (b) 80 × 50 = 4,000
    (c) Yes
```
          2
        8 4
    ×   5 2
      1 6 8
    4 2 0
    4, 3 6 8
```

45. (a) 38,037
    (b) 400 × 90 = 36,000
    (c) Yes
```
          8
          2
        4 0 9
    ×     9 3
      1 2 2 7
    3 6 8 1
    3 8, 0 3 7
```

46. (a) 37,088
    (b) 1,000 × 40 = 40,000
    (c) Yes
```
          2
        6 1
        4
        9 7 6
    ×     3 8
      7 8 0 8
    2 9 2 8
    3 7, 0 8 8
```

47. (a) 5 R 3
       43 ÷ 8 = 5 R 3
    (b) 40 ÷ 8 = 5
    (c) Yes

48. (a) 89 R 4
    (b) 540 ÷ 6 = 90
    (c) Yes
```
          8 9
  6 ) 5 3 8
      4 8
        5 8
        5 4
          4
```

49. (a) 2,191 R 1
    (b) 8,800 ÷ 4 = 2,200
    (c) Yes
```
        2, 1 9 1
  4 ) 8, 7 6 5
      8
        7
        4
        3 6
        3 6
            5
            4
            1
```

50.

12 × 255 = 3,060

```
        1   1
        2 5 5
    ×     1 2
        5 1 0
        2 5 5
      3, 0 6 0
```

There are **3,060** balloons in a dozen packets.

51.

$2,275 \div 7 = 325$
$3 \times 325 = 975$

It makes **975** watches in 3 days.

52.

$4 \times \$253 = \$1,012$
$3 \times \$78 = \$234$
$\$1,012 + \$234 = \$1,246$
He spent **\$1,246** altogether.

53.

$\$276 \div 4 = \$69$
$7 \times \$69 = \$483$
Anna spends **\$483** on the bag and 3 dresses.

54.

$4 \times 35 = 140$
$140 + 219 = 359$
Jason had **359** marbles to begin with.

55.

$114 + 686 = 800$
$800 \times \$17 = \$13,600$
\$13,600 was collected in all.

56.

$7 \times 840 = 5,880$
He bakes 5,880 loaves of bread in a week.

$6 \times 5,880 = 35,280$
He will bake **35,280** loaves of bread in 6 weeks.

57.

$7 \times 50 = 350$
$896 - 350 = 546$
$546 \div 3 = 182$
There are **182** stickers in each album.

58. (a) $25 \times 400 = 10,000$
The principal bought **10,000** pieces of candy altogether.

(b) $2,000 \times 7 = 14,000$
$14,000 - 10,000 = 4,000$
$4,000 \div 400 = 40 \div 4 = 10$

If each child was given 7 pieces, **10** more packages of candy were needed.

59. Use 'Guess and Check' method.

Guess	Her mother's age	Kimi's age	Is her mother 5 times as old as Helen?
1	$44 - 4 = 40$	$16 - 4 = 12$	$40 \div 12 = 3 \text{ R } 4$
2	$44 - 8 = 36$	$16 - 8 = 8$	$36 \div 8 = 4 \text{ R } 4$
3	$44 - 9 = 35$	$16 - 9 = 7$	$35 \div 7 = 5$

Kimi's mother was five times as old as Helen **9** years ago.

60.

$5 \times \$328 = \$1,640$
$\$1,640 \div 8 = \$205$

He must pay **\$205** for them each month.

61.

$\$3,600 - \$320 = \$3,280$

$\$3,280 \div 2 = \$1,640$
Cynthia had \$1,640.

$\$3,600 + \$1,640 = \$5,240$
The total amount of money they had was **\$5,240** in the beginning.

62.

$\$4 \div 2 = \$2$
Each pen cost \$2.
$\$12 - (4 \times \$2) = \$4$
The cost of the book was **\$4**.

63. $250 \times \$12 = \$3,000$
\$3,000 was collected from the sale of all the adult tickets.
$\$6,915 - \$3,000 = \$3,915$
$\$3,915 \div \$9 = 435$
435 children went to the zoo.

64. $\$1,350 - \$400 = \$950$
Each of his six children received \$950.
$\$2,000 + (6 \times \$950) + \$1,350$
$= \$2,000 + \$5,700 + \$1,350$
$= \$9,050$
His bonus was **\$9,050**.

Unit 4: Line Graphs and Tables

1. **11 birds**
$30 - 8 - 3 - 8 = 11$
2. **birds**
Mario saw 11 birds in the park.
3. **cats**
Mario saw 3 cats in the park.

4. **3 more birds**
   $11 - 8 = 3$

5. **18 animals**
   $3 + 5 + 4 = 12$
   $30 - 12 = 18$

6.
Months	Number of mobile phones sold
November	65
December	30
January	75
February	50
March	40

7. **January**
   He sold 75 mobile phones in January.

8. **20 more mobile phones**
   $50 - 30 = 20$

9. **140 mobile phones**
   $75 + 65 = 140$

10. **80 mobile phones**
    $40 \times 2 = 80$

11. **$9,180**
    $50 + 40 = 90$
    $90 \times \$102 = \$9,180$

12. **150 students**

13. **2006**
    250 students took the school bus in 2006.

14. **100 students**
    $225 - 125 = 100$

15. **125 students**
    $250 - 125 = 125$

16. **750 students**
    $250 + 150 + 125 + 225 = 750$

17.
Name	Amount of money collected
Mandy	**$270**
Kim	**$140**
Felix	**$260**
Ratana	**$200**
Robert	**$130**
Janice	**$140**

18. **Mandy** and **Felix**
    Mandy collected $270 and Felix collected $260.

19. **Kim** and **Janice**
    Both collected $140.

20. **Felix**
    $\$130 \times 2 = \$260$

21. **$1,140**
    $\$270 + \$140 + \$260 + \$200 + \$130 + \$140 = \$1,140$

22. **$860**
    $\$2,000 - \$1,140 = \$860$

23. **3rd week**
    There were 500 visitors in the 3rd week.

24. **2,250 visitors**
    $2,750 - 500 = 2,250$

25. **1,750 visitors**
    $3,500 - 1,750 = 1,750$

26. **3,000 visitors**
    $3,500 - 500 = 3,000$

27. **$76,500**
    $3,500 + 1,750 + 500 + 2,750 = 8,500$
    $8,500 \times \$9 = \$76,500$

Review 2

1. **(4)**
   $$\begin{array}{r} 943 \\ \times\ \ 57 \\ \hline 6601 \\ 4715\ \ \\ \hline 53,751 \end{array}$$

2. **(4)**
   $$\begin{array}{r} 725 \\ 10\overline{)7,256} \\ 70\ \ \ \ \\ \hline 25\ \ \\ 20\ \ \\ \hline 56 \\ 50 \\ \hline 6 \end{array}$$

3. **(2)**
   $140 + 142 + 136 = 418$
   $557 - 418 = 139$ cm

4. **(2)**
   $139 - 136 = 3$ cm

5. **(3)**
   Felicia's test score in mathematics in March was 55.

6. **(2)**
   $80 - 70 = 10$

7. **(1)**
   Felicia scored 80 in mathematics in February.

8. **416**
   $\square \div 8 = 52$
   $\square = 52 \times 8 = 416$

9. **5,400**
   $1,785 \times 3 \approx 1,800 \times 3 = 5,400$

10. **1,530 R 3**
    $$\begin{array}{r} 1,530 \\ 4\overline{)6,123} \\ 4\ \ \ \ \ \\ \hline 21\ \ \ \\ 20\ \ \ \\ \hline 12\ \\ 12\ \\ \hline 3 \\ 0 \\ \hline 3 \end{array}$$

11. **250 Indonesian stamps**
    $394 + 125 + 178 = 697$
    $947 - 697 = 250$

12. **629 coins**
    $127 + 245 + 169 + 88 = 629$

13. **318 more stamps**
    $947 - 629 = 318$

14. **17,015**
    $$\begin{array}{r} 205 \\ \times\ \ 83 \\ \hline 615 \\ 1640\ \ \\ \hline 17,015 \end{array}$$

15. **989**
    $$\begin{array}{r} 989 \\ 8\overline{)7,916} \\ 72\ \ \ \\ \hline 71\ \ \\ 64\ \ \\ \hline 76 \\ 72 \\ \hline 4 \end{array}$$

16. Bigger box: 120, Smaller box: ?, total 900
    $900 - 120 = 780$
    $780 \div 2 = 390$
    There were **390** pens in the smaller box.

17. $36 \times \$159 = \$5,724$
    $\$8,000 - \$5,724 = \$2,276$
    He earned **$2,276**.

18.

1,230

Tai
Reta
Veronica

?

$1,230 \div 6 = 205$
$205 \times 9 = 1,845$
The three children have **1,845** beads altogether.

19. $3,000 - 54 = 2,946$
$2,946 \times \$9 = \$26,514$
The publisher made **$26,514** from the sale of the books.

20. (a)

?

| 1,395 | 1,395 | 1,395 | 1,395 | 1,395 | 1,395 | 1,395 | 1,395 |

$8 \times 1,395 = 11,160$
The factory can make **11,160** remote-controlled cars in eight weeks.

(b)

40,455

| ? | ? | ? | ? | ? | ? | ? | ? | ? |

$40,455 \div 9 = 4,495$
The factory must make **4,495** remote-controlled cars in a week.

Unit 5: Fractions

1. $3\frac{1}{2}$
2. $6\frac{2}{3}$
3. $5\frac{1}{4}$
4. $9\frac{1}{12}$
5. $7\frac{5}{7}$
6. $4\frac{5}{8}$
7. $1\frac{4}{9}$
8. $2\frac{3}{5}$
9. $8\frac{1}{6}$
10. $3\frac{9}{11}$
11. $2, 3, 2\frac{3}{5}$
12. $4, 6, 4\frac{6}{7}$
13. $8, 3, 8\frac{3}{8}$
14. $3, 1, 3\frac{1}{6}$
15. $6, 7, 6\frac{7}{12}$
16. $2\frac{3}{5}, 3\frac{2}{5}, 4\frac{4}{5}$
17. $1\frac{3}{9} / 1\frac{1}{3}, 1\frac{8}{9}, 2\frac{7}{9}$
18. $6\frac{4}{7}, 7\frac{1}{7}, 7\frac{4}{7}$
19. **4**
   1 whole = 2 halves
   $2 \times 2 = 4$
20. **10**
   1 whole = 3 thirds
   $(3 \times 3) + 1 = 10$
21. **62**
   1 whole = 11 elevenths
   $(5 \times 11) + 7 = 62$
22. **21**
   1 whole = 12 twelfths
   $(1 \times 12) + 9 = 21$
23. **61**
   1 whole = 7 sevenths
   $(8 \times 7) + 5 = 61$
24. **19**
   1 whole = 4 quarters
   $4\frac{3}{4} = (4 \times 4) + 3 = 19$
25. **11**
   1 whole = 6 sixths
   $(1 \times 6) + 5 = 11$
26. **75**
   1 whole = 8 eighths
   $(9 \times 8) + 3 = 75$
27. **67**
   1 whole = 10 tenths
   $(6 \times 10) + 7 = 67$
28. $\frac{1}{2}, \frac{5}{4}, \frac{9}{4}$
29. $\frac{4}{7}, 1, \frac{9}{7}$
30. $\frac{1}{5}, \frac{6}{5}, 2$
31. $1\frac{1}{2} = \frac{2}{2} + \frac{1}{2} = \frac{3}{2}$
32. $1\frac{3}{10} = \frac{10}{10} + \frac{3}{10} = \frac{13}{10}$
33. $2\frac{3}{4} = \frac{8}{4} + \frac{3}{4} = \frac{11}{4}$
34. $4\frac{3}{5} = \frac{20}{5} + \frac{3}{5} = \frac{23}{5}$
35. $7\frac{1}{6} = \frac{42}{6} + \frac{1}{6} = \frac{43}{6}$
36. $8\frac{2}{3} = \frac{24}{3} + \frac{2}{3} = \frac{26}{3}$
37. $3\frac{5}{8} = \frac{24}{8} + \frac{5}{8} = \frac{29}{8}$
38. $3\frac{7}{12} = \frac{36}{12} + \frac{7}{12} = \frac{43}{12}$
39. $8\frac{4}{9} = \frac{72}{9} + \frac{4}{9} = \frac{76}{9}$
40. $2\frac{4}{7} = \frac{14}{7} + \frac{4}{7} = \frac{18}{7}$
41. $\frac{11}{2} = \frac{10}{2} + \frac{1}{2} = 5 + \frac{1}{2} = 5\frac{1}{2}$
42. $\frac{9}{4} = \frac{8}{4} + \frac{1}{4} = 2 + \frac{1}{4} = 2\frac{1}{4}$
43. $\frac{5}{5} = 1$
44. $\frac{16}{2} = 8$
45. $\frac{37}{5} = \frac{35}{5} + \frac{2}{5} = 7 + \frac{2}{5} = 7\frac{2}{5}$
46. $\frac{12}{3} = 4$
47. $\frac{15}{8} = \frac{8}{8} + \frac{7}{8} = 1 + \frac{7}{8} = 1\frac{7}{8}$
48. $\frac{17}{6} = \frac{12}{6} + \frac{5}{6} = 2 + \frac{5}{6} = 2\frac{5}{6}$

Singapore Math Level 4A & 4B

49. $\frac{23}{6} = \frac{18}{6} + \frac{5}{6} = 3 + \frac{5}{6} = 3\frac{5}{6}$

50. $\frac{38}{9} = \frac{36}{9} + \frac{2}{9} = 4 + \frac{2}{9} = 4\frac{2}{9}$

51. $\frac{2}{5} + \frac{4}{5} = \frac{6}{5} = 1\frac{1}{5}$

52. $\frac{2}{3} + \frac{4}{9} = \frac{6}{9} + \frac{4}{9} = \frac{10}{9} = 1\frac{1}{9}$

53. $\frac{3}{7} + \frac{13}{14} = \frac{6}{14} + \frac{13}{14} = \frac{19}{14} = 1\frac{5}{14}$

54. $\frac{5}{8} + \frac{3}{4} = \frac{5}{8} + \frac{6}{8} = \frac{11}{8} = 1\frac{3}{8}$

55. $\frac{7}{12} + \frac{2}{6} + \frac{9}{12} = \frac{7}{12} + \frac{4}{12} + \frac{9}{12} = \frac{20}{12} = 1\frac{2}{3}$

56. $\frac{1}{2} + \frac{3}{10} + \frac{9}{10} = \frac{5}{10} + \frac{3}{10} + \frac{9}{10} = \frac{17}{10} = 1\frac{7}{10}$

57. $\frac{2}{4} + \frac{7}{8} + \frac{1}{4} = \frac{4}{8} + \frac{7}{8} + \frac{2}{8} = \frac{13}{8} = 1\frac{5}{8}$

58. $\frac{1}{3} + \frac{3}{9} + \frac{5}{9} = \frac{3}{9} + \frac{3}{9} + \frac{5}{9} = \frac{11}{9} = 1\frac{2}{9}$

59. $6 - \frac{2}{8} = \frac{48}{8} - \frac{2}{8} = \frac{46}{8} = 5\frac{6}{8} = 5\frac{3}{4}$

60. $10 - \frac{5}{12} = \frac{120}{12} - \frac{5}{12} = \frac{115}{12} = 9\frac{7}{12}$

61. $\frac{8}{9} - \frac{2}{9} = \frac{6}{9} = \frac{2}{3}$

62. $\frac{9}{10} - \frac{1}{2} = \frac{9}{10} - \frac{5}{10} = \frac{4}{10} = \frac{2}{5}$

63. $2\frac{6}{9} - \frac{1}{3} = 2\frac{6}{9} - \frac{3}{9} = 2\frac{3}{9} = 2\frac{1}{3}$

64. $4\frac{9}{12} - \frac{2}{4} = 4\frac{9}{12} - \frac{6}{12} = 4\frac{3}{12} = 4\frac{1}{4}$

65. $5\frac{7}{12} - \frac{1}{4} = 5\frac{7}{12} - \frac{3}{12} = 5\frac{4}{12} = 5\frac{1}{3}$

66. $7 - \frac{9}{10} - \frac{2}{5} = \frac{70}{10} - \frac{9}{10} - \frac{4}{10} = \frac{57}{10} = 5\frac{7}{10}$

67. $\frac{2}{\cancel{3}} \times \cancel{21}^{7} = 14$

68. $\frac{1}{\cancel{8}} \times \cancel{72}^{9} = 9$

69. $\frac{5}{\cancel{9}} \times \cancel{81}^{9} = 45$

70. $\frac{4}{\cancel{5}} \times \cancel{65}^{13} = 52$

71. $\frac{9}{\cancel{10}} \times \cancel{20}^{2} = 18$

72. $\frac{5}{\cancel{6}} \times \cancel{48}^{8} = 40$

73. $\frac{3}{\cancel{7}} \times \cancel{63}^{9} = 27$

74. $\frac{3}{\cancel{4}} \times \cancel{52}^{13} = 39$

75. $\frac{4}{\cancel{9}} \times \cancel{27}^{3} = 12$

76. $\frac{1}{\cancel{6}} \times \cancel{84}^{14} = 14$

77. $1 - \frac{3}{8} = \frac{8}{8} - \frac{3}{8} = \frac{5}{8}$

She had $\frac{5}{8}$ of the cake left.

78. $\frac{7}{12} - \frac{1}{6} = \frac{7}{12} - \frac{2}{12} = \frac{5}{12}$

The mass of the sand in the can is $\frac{5}{12}$ lb.

79. $\frac{5}{6} + \frac{1}{10} + \frac{9}{10} = \frac{50}{60} + \frac{6}{60} + \frac{54}{60}$
$= \frac{110}{60} = 1\frac{50}{60} = 1\frac{5}{6}$

The total mass of the three boxes is $1\frac{5}{6}$ kg.

80. $\frac{1}{4} + \frac{5}{12} = \frac{3}{12} + \frac{5}{12} = \frac{8}{12}$
$\frac{11}{12} - \frac{8}{12} = \frac{3}{12} = \frac{1}{4}$

The length of ribbon Mrs. Kwan cut was $\frac{1}{4}$ m.

81. $\frac{1}{3} + \frac{5}{9} = \frac{3}{9} + \frac{5}{9} = \frac{8}{9}$
$1\frac{2}{3} - \frac{8}{9} = \frac{5}{3} - \frac{8}{9} = \frac{15}{9} - \frac{8}{9} = \frac{7}{9}$

Lina prepared $\frac{7}{9}$ L of fruit punch.

82. $\frac{6}{10} - \frac{1}{2} = \frac{6}{10} - \frac{5}{10} = \frac{1}{10}$
$\frac{6}{10} + \frac{1}{10} = \frac{7}{10}$

The two children drank $\frac{7}{10}$ L of milk in all.

83. $\frac{1}{4} + \frac{1}{8} = \frac{2}{8} + \frac{1}{8} = \frac{3}{8}$
$5 - \frac{3}{8} = \frac{40}{8} - \frac{3}{8} = \frac{37}{8} = 4\frac{5}{8}$

She had $4\frac{5}{8}$ L of cooking oil left.

84. $\frac{3}{4} + \frac{3}{8} = \frac{6}{8} + \frac{3}{8} = \frac{9}{8}$
$12\frac{7}{8} - \frac{9}{8} = 12\frac{7}{8} - 1\frac{1}{8} = 11\frac{6}{8} = 11\frac{3}{4}$

She cycled $11\frac{3}{4}$ km.

85. $16 + 24 + 20 = 60$
There are 60 beads in a box.
$\frac{20}{60} = \frac{1}{3}$
$\frac{1}{3}$ of the beads in the box are blue.

86.
18 mi.
$\frac{1}{\cancel{6}} \times \cancel{18}^{3} = 3$ mi.

$3 \times 5 = 15$ mi.
He has to travel **15 miles** in order to reach Town B.

87.
32
$32 \div 8 = 4$
$3 \times 4 = 12$
Tara ate **12** chocolates.

88.
50

231

Singapore Math Level 4A & 4B

(a) $28 + 15 + 7 = 50$
Farmer Bill had 50 birds.
$50 \div 5 = 10$
$4 \times 10 = 40$
He sold **40** birds in all.

(b) $28 - 12 = 16$
He had 16 chickens left.
$\frac{16}{28} = \frac{4}{7}$
$\frac{4}{7}$ of the chickens were left.

89. $1 - \frac{5}{8} - \frac{1}{4} = \frac{8}{8} - \frac{5}{8} - \frac{2}{8} = \frac{1}{8}$

$\frac{1}{\cancel{8}_1} \times \cancel{568}^{71} = 71$

There were **71** children at the concert.

90. $\frac{2}{3} \,\square\, \$60$

$\frac{1}{3} \,\square\, \$60 \div 2 = \$30$

$3 \times \$30 = \$90$
Isabel received **$90**.

Unit 6: Angles

1. $\angle ABC = \angle \mathbf{y}$
$\angle ACB = \angle \mathbf{x}$
$\angle BAC = \angle \mathbf{z}$

2. $\angle d = \angle \mathbf{SRQ}\ /\ \angle \mathbf{QRS}$
$\angle e = \angle \mathbf{OSR}\ /\ \angle \mathbf{RSO}$
$\angle f = \angle \mathbf{SOP}\ /\ \angle \mathbf{POS}$
$\angle g = \angle \mathbf{OPQ}\ /\ \angle \mathbf{QPO}$
$\angle h = \angle \mathbf{PQR}\ /\ \angle \mathbf{RQP}$

3. $\angle \mathbf{b}, \angle \mathbf{c}, \angle \mathbf{d}, \angle \mathbf{f}$

4. $\angle \mathbf{a}, \angle \mathbf{e}$

	Estimated value	Actual measurement
5.	$\angle a = 100°$	$\angle a = \mathbf{98°}$
6.	$\angle b = 70°$	$\angle b = \mathbf{62°}$
7.	$\angle PQR = 100°$	$\angle PQR = \mathbf{105°}$
8.	$\angle XWY = 120°$	$\angle XWY = \mathbf{126°}$

9.

10.

11.

12.

13. $\frac{1}{4}$ / quarter

14. **180**

15. $\frac{3}{4}$ / three-quarter

16. **4**

17. $\frac{1}{2}$ / Half

18. $\frac{1}{4}$ / Quarter

19. Tony: **north**
Aaron: **northeast**
Susan: **east**
Jasmin: **southeast**
Maggie: **south**
Sam: **southwest**
Malik: **west**
Zack: **northwest**

20. (a) **northwest**
(b) **southeast**
(c) **west**
(d) **east**
(e) **north**
(f) **east**
(g) **northeast**
(h) **southwest**

21. (a) **225**
(b) **180**
(c) **270**
(d) **45**
(e) $\frac{1}{4}$ / quarter
(f) $\frac{3}{4}$ / three-quarter

Review 3

1. **(3)**
$6\frac{7}{9} = \frac{54}{9} + \frac{7}{9} = \frac{61}{9}$

2. **(4)**
$\frac{2}{5} - \frac{3}{10} = \frac{4}{10} - \frac{3}{10} = \frac{1}{10}$

3. **(4)**
$\frac{4}{9} + \frac{2}{3} = \frac{4}{9} + \frac{6}{9} = \frac{10}{9} = \frac{9}{9} + \frac{1}{9} = 1\frac{1}{9}$

4. **(4)**
$\dfrac{\text{Shaded triangles}}{\text{Total triangles}} = \frac{7}{12}$

5. **(1)**
$\frac{2}{\cancel{7}_1} \times \cancel{98}^{14} = 28$

6. **(3)**
1 whole = 6 sixths
$(5 \times 6) + 1 = 31$

7. **(3)**
$\angle a = 18°$

8. $32\frac{2}{6} = \mathbf{32\frac{1}{3}}$

9. $\frac{24}{5} = \frac{20}{5} + \frac{4}{5} = \mathbf{4\frac{4}{5}}$

Singapore Math Level 4A & 4B

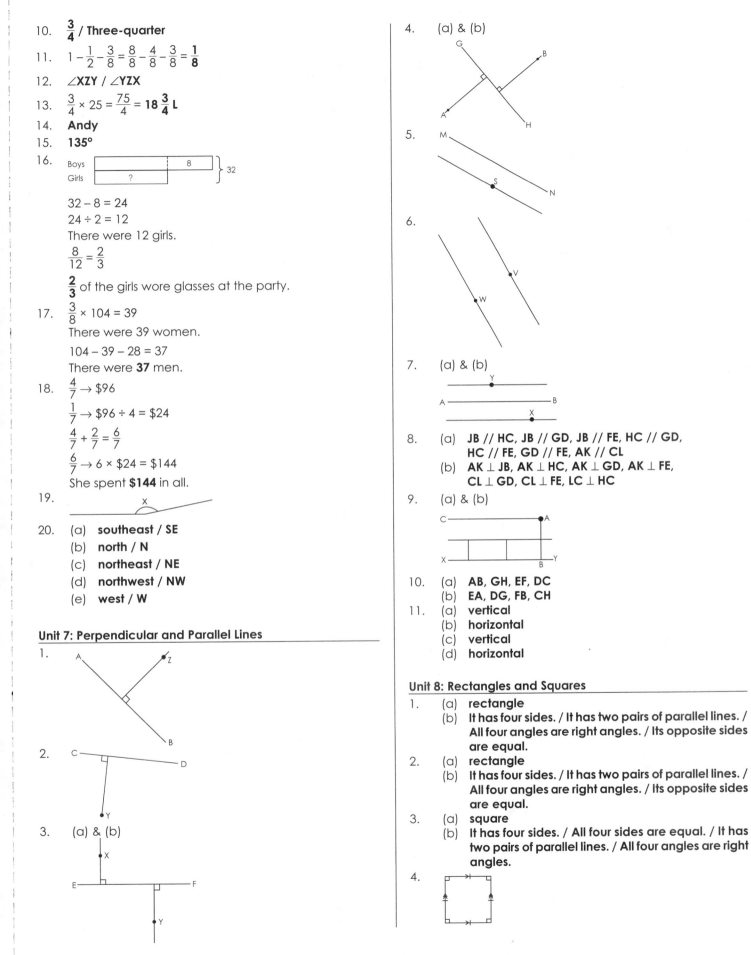

10. $\frac{3}{4}$ / Three-quarter

11. $1 - \frac{1}{2} - \frac{3}{8} = \frac{8}{8} - \frac{4}{8} - \frac{3}{8} = \frac{1}{8}$

12. $\angle$**XZY** / $\angle$**YZX**

13. $\frac{3}{4} \times 25 = \frac{75}{4} = \mathbf{18 \frac{3}{4} L}$

14. **Andy**

15. **135°**

16.

Boys		8	⎫
Girls	?		⎭ 32

   $32 - 8 = 24$
   $24 \div 2 = 12$
   There were 12 girls.
   $\frac{8}{12} = \frac{2}{3}$
   $\frac{2}{3}$ of the girls wore glasses at the party.

17. $\frac{3}{8} \times 104 = 39$
   There were 39 women.
   $104 - 39 - 28 = 37$
   There were **37** men.

18. $\frac{4}{7} \to \$96$
   $\frac{1}{7} \to \$96 \div 4 = \$24$
   $\frac{4}{7} + \frac{2}{7} = \frac{6}{7}$
   $\frac{6}{7} \to 6 \times \$24 = \$144$
   She spent **$144** in all.

19.

20. (a) **southeast / SE**
    (b) **north / N**
    (c) **northeast / NE**
    (d) **northwest / NW**
    (e) **west / W**

Unit 7: Perpendicular and Parallel Lines

1.

2.

3. (a) & (b)

4. (a) & (b)

5.

6.

7. (a) & (b)

8. (a) **JB // HC, JB // GD, JB // FE, HC // GD,**
    HC // FE, GD // FE, AK // CL
   (b) **AK $\perp$ JB, AK $\perp$ HC, AK $\perp$ GD, AK $\perp$ FE,**
    CL $\perp$ GD, CL $\perp$ FE, LC $\perp$ HC

9. (a) & (b)

10. (a) **AB, GH, EF, DC**
    (b) **EA, DG, FB, CH**

11. (a) **vertical**
    (b) **horizontal**
    (c) **vertical**
    (d) **horizontal**

Unit 8: Rectangles and Squares

1. (a) **rectangle**
   (b) **It has four sides. / It has two pairs of parallel lines. /**
    All four angles are right angles. / Its opposite sides
    are equal.

2. (a) **rectangle**
   (b) **It has four sides. / It has two pairs of parallel lines. /**
    All four angles are right angles. / Its opposite sides
    are equal.

3. (a) **square**
   (b) **It has four sides. / All four sides are equal. / It has**
    two pairs of parallel lines. / All four angles are right
    angles.

4.

Singapore Math Level 4A & 4B

5.

6. x = **12**
   y = **5**
7. x = 40 ÷ 5 = **8**
   y = **40**
8. x = **10**
   y = **10**
9. 90° − 15° = **75°**
10. 90° − 25° − 18° = **47°**
11. 90° − 62° − 8° = **20°**
12. 90° − 67° − 10° = **13°**
13. 90° − 31° − 13° = **46°**
14. AB = 5 + 8 + 5 = **18 in.**
    AH = **8 in.**
    AH has the same length as BC.
15. DF = 10 + 10 + 15 = **35 cm**
    EF = 10 + 15 = **25 cm**
16. EF = 32 − 11 − 4 = **17 ft.**
    DE = 21 − 8 − 5 = **8 ft.**
17. ML = (16 + 8) − 16 = **8 cm**
    AB = 16 + 8 + 8 = **32 cm**
18. BC = 18 − 8 − 6 = **4 in.**
    EF = 33 − 15 = **18 in.**

Review 4

1. **(1)**
2. **(2)**

3. **(1)**
   17 − 3 = 14 cm
4. **(1)**
   90° − 26° − 48° = 16°
5. **(3)**
   48 ÷ 2 = 24 cm
6. **(3)**
   24 − 13 = 11 cm
7. **(2)**
8. **(3)**
9. **(1)**

10. **(2)**
    There are 3 horizontal lines in the figure.
11. **EF**
12. **36°**
    90° − 18° = 72°
    72° ÷ 2 = 36°
13. **It has four sides. / All four sides are equal. / It has two pairs of parallel lines. / All four angles are right angles.**

14. **25 in.**
    108 − 83 = 25 in.
15. **AH // DE** and **AH // FG**
16. (a) **parallel / vertical**
    (b) **parallel / horizontal**
17. (a) **horizontal**
    (b) **vertical**
18. **BC**
19.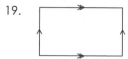

20. *Accept other correct answers.*

Mid-Review

1. **(4)**
   1,500 + 86,576 = 88,076
2. **(3)**
   The number 0 is in the hundreds place.
3. **(2)**
4. **(3)**
   2 × 33 = 66
   3 × 22 = 66
   6 × 11 = 66
5. **(3)**
   9,004 ≈ 9,000
6. **(4)**
   $3\frac{2}{5} = \frac{15}{5} + \frac{2}{5} = \frac{17}{5}$
7. **(2)**
   $$\begin{array}{r} 3\,9\,{}^{7}0\,{}^{3}4 \\ \times \qquad 8 \\ \hline 3\,1,2\,3\,2 \end{array}$$
8. **(4)**
   1 whole = 4 quarters
   (5 × 4) + 3 = 23
9. **(3)**

   | Thursday | 1,659 |
   | Friday | 1,659 | 1,659 | 1,659 |

   4 × 1,659 = 6,636
10. **(4)**
    $40 + $10 = $50
    Anya had $50 at first.
    $\frac{40}{50} = \frac{4}{5}$
11. **(4)**
    90 + 81 + 75 = 246
12. **(4)**
    90 − 63 = 27

13. **(2)**

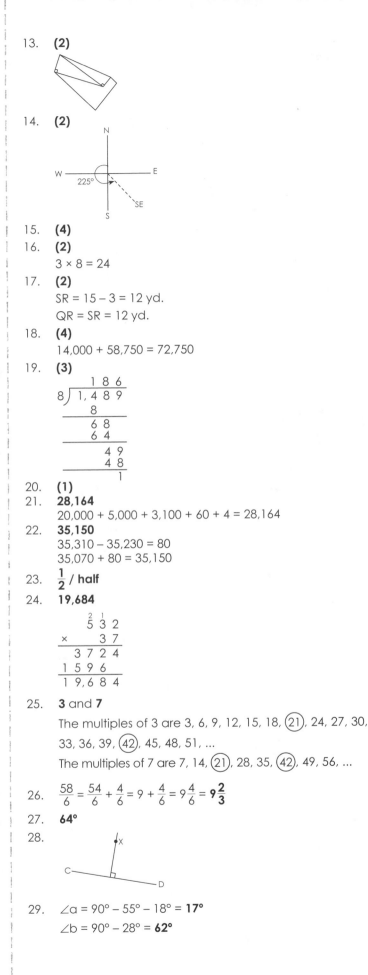

14. **(2)**

15. **(4)**

16. **(2)**

$3 \times 8 = 24$

17. **(2)**

SR = 15 − 3 = 12 yd.

QR = SR = 12 yd.

18. **(4)**

14,000 + 58,750 = 72,750

19. **(3)**

```
      1 8 6
8 ) 1, 4 8 9
    8
    6 8
    6 4
      4 9
      4 8
        1
```

20. **(1)**

21. **28,164**

20,000 + 5,000 + 3,100 + 60 + 4 = 28,164

22. **35,150**

35,310 − 35,230 = 80

35,070 + 80 = 35,150

23. $\frac{1}{2}$ / **half**

24. **19,684**

```
        2 1
      5 3 2
  ×     3 7
    3 7 2 4
  1 5 9 6
  1 9, 6 8 4
```

25. **3** and **7**

The multiples of 3 are 3, 6, 9, 12, 15, 18, ㉑, 24, 27, 30, 33, 36, 39, ㊷, 45, 48, 51, ...

The multiples of 7 are 7, 14, ㉑, 28, 35, ㊷, 49, 56, ...

26. $\frac{58}{6} = \frac{54}{6} + \frac{4}{6} = 9 + \frac{4}{6} = 9\frac{4}{6} = \mathbf{9\frac{2}{3}}$

27. **64°**

28.

29. $\angle a = 90° - 55° - 18° = \mathbf{17°}$

$\angle b = 90° - 28° = \mathbf{62°}$

30. $3 + \frac{2}{5} + \frac{9}{10} = 3 + \frac{4}{10} + \frac{9}{10} = 3\frac{13}{10} = \mathbf{4\frac{3}{10}}$

31.

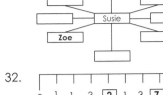

32.

0 $\frac{1}{10}$ $\frac{1}{5}$ $\frac{3}{10}$ $\boxed{\frac{2}{5}}$ $\frac{1}{2}$ $\frac{3}{5}$ $\boxed{\frac{7}{10}}$ $\frac{4}{5}$ $\boxed{\frac{9}{10}}$ 1

33.

Day	Number of pots of flowers
Monday	16
Tuesday	12
Wednesday	18
Thursday	20
Friday	24

34. **90**

16 + 12 + 18 + 20 + 24 = 90

35. $421 \div 8 \approx 400 \div 8 = \mathbf{50}$

36. **2**

37. **187**

□ ÷ 7 = 26 R 5

□ = 7 × 26 + 5 = 187

38. **2 lb.**

$1 - \frac{5}{6} = \frac{1}{6}$

$\frac{1}{\cancel{6}_1} \times \cancel{12}^{2} = 2$

39. $9,055 \times 7 \approx 9,000 \times 7 = \mathbf{63,000}$

40.

270°

41. $8 \times \$630 = \$5,040$

$295 + $1,853 = $2,148

$5,040 − $2,148 = $2,892

The cost of the television set was **$2,892**.

42.

book ?

soccer ball $15

car $15 $198 $230

$230 − $198 − $15 − $17

The cost of the book is **$17**.

43. $\frac{1}{4} + \frac{1}{8} = \frac{2}{8} + \frac{1}{8} = \frac{3}{8}$

Singapore Math Level 4A & 4B

Juan ate $\frac{3}{8}$ of the pizza.

$1 - \frac{1}{4} - \frac{3}{8} = \frac{8}{8} - \frac{2}{8} - \frac{3}{8} = \frac{3}{8}$

Cindy ate $\frac{3}{8}$ of the pizza.

44. $\frac{3}{\overset{\displaystyle8}{1}} \times \overset{7}{56} = 21$

Esther gave 21 stickers to her sister.

$56 - 21 - 18 = 17$

She gave **17** stickers to her friend.

45. Use 'Guess and Check' method.

Guess	Mr. Popovic's age	Granddaughter's age	Is Mr. Popovic 5 times as old as her granddaughter?
1	78	14	No 78 ÷ 14 = 5 R 8
2	80	16	Yes 80 ÷ 16 = 5

Mr. Popovic will be five times as old as his granddaughter in **4** years' time.

Challenge Questions

1.

Day	1	2	3	4	5	6	7	8
No. of eggs sold	15	25	**36**	48	61	**75**	90	**106**

+10 +11 +12 +13 +14 +15 +16

2.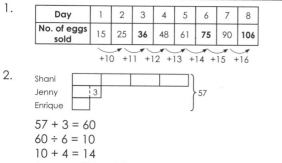

$57 + 3 = 60$
$60 \div 6 = 10$
$10 + 4 = 14$
Jenny will be **14** years old in four years.

3. Use 'Guess and Check' method.

A	B	A ÷ B	Check
29	5	$5\frac{4}{5}$	☞
29	4	$7\frac{1}{4}$	☞
28	5	$5\frac{3}{5}$	☞
28	4	7	☞
26	4	$6\frac{1}{2}$	☞
25	4	$6\frac{1}{4}$	☞

A is **25** and B is **4**.

4. second digit: $3 \times 3 = 9$
fourth digit: $2 \times 3 = 6$
third digit: $9 - 6 = 3$
first digit: $9 - 2 = 7$
last digit: $7 - 2 = 5$
I am **79,365**.

5. Use 'Guess and Check' method.

X	Y	product	sum
10	40	10 × 40 = 400	10 + 40 = 50
20	30	20 × 30 = 600	20 + 30 = 50

X is **20** and Y is **30**.

6. $6 \times 10 = 60$
Jason's score in the test was 60.

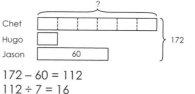

$172 - 60 = 112$
$112 \div 7 = 16$
$6 \times 16 = 96$
Chet's score in the test was **96**.

7. Use 'Guess and Check' method.

Number 1	Number 2	Quotient	Difference	Check
10	120	12	110	☞
11	132	12	121	☞
12	144	12	132	☞

The two numbers are **12** and **144** respectively.

8.

Week	1	2	3	4	5	6	7	8
Savings	$2	$4	$6	$8	$10	$12	$14	$16

$\$2 + \$4 + \$6 + \$8 + \$10 + \$12 + \$14 + \$16 = \$72$
The bag costs **$72**.

9. Factors of 8 are 1, 2, 4, and 8.
$1st \times 4th = 4 \times 8 = 32$
1st digit: 8 (the largest single digit for factors of 8)
4th digit: 4 ($32 \div 8 = 4$)
2nd digit: 1 ($4 - 3 = 1$)
3rd digit: 2
1 am **8,124**.

10. First six multiples of 6 are 6, 12, 18, 24, 30, and 36.
10th multiple of 6 is 60.
11th multiple of 6 is 66.

6	30	24	6 + 30 + 24 = 60
18	12	36	18 + 12 + 36 = 66

11.

$7 \times \$1,255 = \$8,785$
$12 \times \$8,785 = \$105,420$
The three of them earn **$105,420** in a year.

12.

$360° \div 12 = 30°$

When the minute hand moves from one number to the other, it turns 30°.

$5 \times 30° = 150°$

The minute hand will point at 5 when turns 150°.

Sylvia eats her breakfast at **8:25 A.M.**

Singapore Math Level 4A & 4B

Unit 9: Decimals (Part 1)

1. $\frac{4}{10}$ = **0.4**

2. $\frac{6}{10}$ = **0.6**

3. $\frac{2}{10}$ = **0.2**

4. $\frac{7}{10}$ = **0.7**

5. $\frac{1}{10}$ = **0.1**

6. $\frac{7}{10}$ = **0.7**

7. $3\frac{2}{10}$ = **3.2**

8. 13 tenths = 1 one 3 tenths
   $4\frac{13}{10} = 5\frac{3}{10}$ = **5.3**

9. 18 tenths = 1 one 8 tenths
   $2\frac{18}{10} = 3\frac{8}{10}$ = **3.8**

10. 24 tenths = 2 ones 4 tenths
    $9\frac{24}{10} = 11\frac{4}{10}$ = **11.4**

11. **9**
    $0.9 = \frac{9}{10}$ = 9 tenths

12. **36**
    $3.6 = 3\frac{6}{10}$ = 3 ones 6 tenths = 36 tenths

13. **784**
    $78.4 = 78\frac{4}{10}$ = 78 ones 4 tenths = 784 tenths

14. **183**
    $18.3 = 18\frac{3}{10}$ = 18 ones 3 tenths = 183 tenths

15. **215**
    $215 = 21\frac{5}{10}$ = 21 ones 5 tenths = 215 tenths

16. **1.4**, **2.9**
    Each marking on the number line is 0.1.

17. **2.7**, **4.8**
    Each marking on the number line is 0.1.

18. **6.9**, **7.6**
    Each marking on the number line is 0.1.

19. **9**
20. **4**
21. **3**
22. **6**
23. **8**
24. (a) **1**
    (b) **tenths**
    (c) **90**
    (d) **1**
25. (a) **5**
    (b) **tenths**
    (c) **7**
    (d) **5 tens/50**

26. $0.26 = \frac{26}{100}$

27. $0.74 = \frac{74}{100}$

28. $0.03 = \frac{3}{100}$

29. $0.62 = \frac{62}{100}$

30. $0.45 = \frac{45}{100}$

31. $\frac{8}{100} = $ **0.08**

32. $\frac{16}{100} = $ **0.16**

33. $\frac{32}{100} = $ **0.32**

34. $\frac{188}{100} = 1 + \frac{88}{100} = $ **1.88**

35. $\frac{311}{100} = 3 + \frac{11}{100} = $ **3.11**

36. **543**

    $5.43 = 5\frac{43}{100} = $ 5 ones 43 hundredths

                   = 543 hundredths

37. **8,195**

    $81.95 = 81\frac{95}{100} = $ 81 ones 95 hundredths

                   = 8,195 hundredths

38. **6,072**

    $60.72 = 60\frac{72}{100} = $ 60 ones 72 hundredths

                   = 6,072 hundredths

39. **3,854**

    $38.54 = 38\frac{54}{100} = $ 38 ones 54 hundredths

                   = 3,854 hundredths

40. **9,045**

    $90.45 = 90\frac{45}{100} = $ 90 ones 45 hundredths

                   = 9,045 hundredths

41. **0.12, 0.25**

    Each marking on the number line is 0.01.

42. **0.57, 0.66**

    Each marking on the number line is 0.01.

43. **0.86, 0.95**

    Each marking on the number line is 0.01.

44. **2, 0, 4, 5**

45. **7, 1, 3, 8**

46. **9, 4, 2, 8**

47. **6, 4, 1, 3**

48. **5, 2, 5, 6**

49. (a) **0**

    (b) **tens**

    (c) **0.2/2 tenths**

    (d) **0.04**

    (e) **70**

50. (a) **1**

    (b) **tens**

    (c) **3/3 ones**

    (d) **0.08**

    (e) **0.1**

51. $\frac{4}{1,000} = $ **0.004**

52. $\frac{15}{1,000} = $ **0.015**

53. $\frac{291}{1,000} = $ **0.291**

54. $\frac{718}{1,000} = $ **0.718**

55. $\frac{1,414}{1,000} = $ **1.414**

56. $\frac{2,086}{1,000} = $ **2.086**

57. **28,404**

    $28.404 = 28\frac{404}{1,000} = $ 28 ones 404 thousandths

                     = 28,404 thousandths

58. **40,687**

    $40.687 = 40\frac{687}{1,000} = $ 40 ones 687 thousandths

                     = 40,687 thousandths

59. **53,936**

    $53.936 = 53\frac{936}{1,000} = $ 53 ones 936 thousandths

                     = 53,936 thousandths

60. **2,308**

    $2.308 = 2\frac{308}{1,000} = $ 2 ones 308 thousandths

                   = 2,308 thousandths

61. **66,799**

    $66.799 = 66\frac{799}{1,000} = $ 66 ones 799 thousandths

                     = 66,799 thousandths

62. **5.008, 5.017**

    Each marking on the number line is 0.001.

63. **9.001, 9.011**

    Each marking on the number line is 0.001.

64. **10.007, 10.014**

    Each marking on the number line is 0.001.

65. **2, 0, 0, 4, 5**

66. **5, 8, 2, 9, 7**

67. **7, 2, 3, 9, 3**

68. **3, 6, 8, 1, 6**

69. **8, 4, 0, 3, 5**

70. (a) **7**

    (b) **tenths**

    (c) **0.08/8 hundredths**

    (d) **0.007**

    (e) **4**

71. (a) **0**

    (b) **thousandths**

    (c) **0.9/9 tenths**

    (d) **10**

    (e) **0.06**

72. **14.4**

73. **78.68**

74. **85.084**

75. **6.5**

76. **57.02**

77. +0.9 +0.9 +0.9 +0.9

    3.8,   4.7,   5.6,   **6.5,**   **7.4**

78.
$$\overset{+0.05}{\frown}\ \overset{+0.05}{\frown}\ \overset{+0.05}{\frown}\ \overset{+0.05}{\frown}$$
15.34, 15.39, 15.44, **15.49, 15.54**

79.
$$\overset{+0.03}{\frown}\ \overset{+0.03}{\frown}\ \overset{+0.03}{\frown}\ \overset{+0.03}{\frown}$$
45.06, 45.09, 45.12, **45.15, 45.18**

80.
$$\overset{+0.001}{\frown}\ \overset{+0.001}{\frown}\ \overset{+0.001}{\frown}\ \overset{+0.001}{\frown}$$
10.088, 10.089, 10.09, **10.091, 10.092**

81.
$$\overset{+0.005}{\frown}\ \overset{+0.005}{\frown}\ \overset{+0.005}{\frown}\ \overset{+0.005}{\frown}$$
82.309, 82.314, 82.319, **82.324, 82.329**

82. **1.8**
Since all have the same ones, compare the tenths. 8 tenths is the largest.

83. **3.65**
$3\frac{605}{1,000} = 3.605 \quad \frac{365}{1,000} = 0.365$
Compare the ones first. Then compare the tenths and hundredths. 3.65 is the largest.

84. **2.91**
$2\frac{901}{1,000} = 2.901 \quad 2\frac{29}{100} = 2.09$
Compare the ones first. Next, compare the tenths and hundredths. Hence, 2.91 is the largest.

85. **7.012**
Since all have the same ones, compare the tenths. Next, compare the hundredths. 0 hundredths is the smallest.

86. $\mathbf{\frac{8,059}{1,000}}$
$8\frac{95}{100} = 8.95 \quad \frac{8,059}{1,000} = 8.059$
Since all have the same ones, compare the tenths. Next, compare the hundredths. 5 hundredths is the smallest.

87. $\mathbf{\frac{399}{1,000}}$
$3\frac{909}{1,000} = 3.909 \quad 3\frac{99}{1,000} = 3.099 \quad \frac{399}{1,000} = 0.399$
Compare the ones first. 0 ones is the smallest.

88. **5.28, 5.028, 2.058**
89. **4.502, 4.25, 4.025**
90. **9.01, 1.09, 0.19**
91. **198.003, 198.03, 198.3**
92. **27.329, 273.29, 2,732.9**
93. **6.017, 6.107, 6.17**
94. $1.04 \approx$ **1**
95. $2.55 \approx$ **3**
96. $15.82 \approx$ **16**
97. $0.95 \approx$ **1**
98. $7.74 \approx$ **8**
99. $1.68 \approx$ **1.7**
100. $33.38 \approx$ **33.4**
101. $2.91 \approx$ **2.9**
102. $14.74 \approx$ **14.7**
103. $6.472 \approx$ **6.5**
104. $89.943 \approx$ **89.9**
105. $10.963 \approx$ **10.96**
106. $59.095 \approx$ **59.10**

107. $7.007 \approx$ **7.01**
108. $0.671 \approx$ **0.67**
109. $2.386 \approx$ **2.39**
110. $15.709 \approx$ **15.71**
111. $\frac{4}{10} =$ **0.4**
112. $\frac{11}{10} = \frac{10}{10} + \frac{1}{10} = 1 + 0.1 =$ **1.1**
113. $5\frac{8}{10} = 5 + \frac{8}{10} = 5 + 0.8 =$ **5.8**
114. $9\frac{4\times2}{5\times2} = 9\frac{8}{10} =$ **9.8**
115. $\frac{1}{100} =$ **0.01**
116. $\frac{28}{100} =$ **0.28**
117. $1\frac{77}{100} =$ **1.77**
118. $4\frac{18\times4}{25\times4} = 4\frac{72}{100} =$ **4.72**
119. $\frac{462}{1,000} =$ **0.462**
120. $\frac{9}{1,000} =$ **0.009**
121. $5\frac{16}{1,000} =$ **5.016**
122. $45\frac{45\times2}{50\times2} = 45\frac{90}{100} =$ **45.9**
123. $6.2 = \frac{62}{10} = 6\frac{2}{10} = \mathbf{6\frac{1}{5}}$
124. $49.4 = \frac{494}{10} = 49\frac{4}{10} = \mathbf{49\frac{2}{5}}$
125. $7.08 = \frac{708}{100} = 7\frac{8}{100} = \mathbf{7\frac{2}{25}}$
126. $51.25 = \frac{5,125}{100} = 51\frac{25}{100} = \mathbf{51\frac{1}{4}}$
127. $1.008 = \frac{1,008}{1,000} = 1\frac{8}{1,000} = \mathbf{1\frac{1}{125}}$
128. $25.42 = \frac{2,542}{100} = 25\frac{42}{100} = \mathbf{25\frac{21}{50}}$

Unit 10: Decimals (Part 2)

1.
```
   0.1
 + 0.3
 -----
   0.4
```

2.
```
   6.2
 + 1.3
 -----
   7.5
```

3.
```
    9.08
 +  5.57
 ------
  14.65
```

4.
```
    5.14
 + 13.63
 ------
  18.77
```

5.
```
   56.01
 + 72.96
 ------
 128.97
```

239

Singapore Math Level 4A & 4B

6.
$$\begin{array}{r} \overset{1}{}\overset{1}{3}9.78 \\ +44.05 \\ \hline \mathbf{83.83} \end{array}$$

7.
$$\begin{array}{r} 0.5 \\ -0.2 \\ \hline \mathbf{0.3} \end{array}$$

8.
$$\begin{array}{r} 9.7 \\ -5.4 \\ \hline \mathbf{4.3} \end{array}$$

9.
$$\begin{array}{r} 4.\overset{5}{8}\overset{11}{1} \\ -2.39 \\ \hline \mathbf{2.22} \end{array}$$

10.
$$\begin{array}{r} \overset{1}{2}\overset{11}{1}.75 \\ -8.03 \\ \hline \mathbf{13.72} \end{array}$$

11.
$$\begin{array}{r} 9\overset{6}{7}.\overset{13}{8}6 \\ -50.72 \\ \hline \mathbf{46.64} \end{array}$$

12.
$$\begin{array}{r} 8\overset{7}{0}.\overset{9}{4}\overset{14}{9} \\ -31.67 \\ \hline \mathbf{48.82} \end{array}$$

13.
$$\begin{array}{r} 5.1 \\ \times2 \\ \hline \mathbf{10.2} \end{array}$$

14.
$$\begin{array}{r} \overset{2}{0}.4 \\ \times5 \\ \hline \mathbf{2.0} \end{array}$$

15.
$$\begin{array}{r} \overset{3}{3}.8 \\ \times4 \\ \hline \mathbf{15.2} \end{array}$$

16.
$$\begin{array}{r} \overset{1}{2}.3 \\ \times6 \\ \hline \mathbf{13.8} \end{array}$$

17.
$$\begin{array}{r} \overset{1}{8}.\overset{4}{1}7 \\ \times7 \\ \hline \mathbf{57.19} \end{array}$$

18.
$$\begin{array}{r} \overset{1}{3}.\overset{1}{4}5 \\ \times3 \\ \hline \mathbf{10.35} \end{array}$$

19.
$$\begin{array}{r} \overset{7}{0}.\overset{7}{7}8 \\ \times9 \\ \hline \mathbf{7.02} \end{array}$$

20.
$$\begin{array}{r} \overset{1}{1}\overset{1}{2}.\overset{3}{3}6 \\ \times5 \\ \hline \mathbf{61.80} \end{array}$$

21.
$$\begin{array}{r} 50.12 \\ \times2 \\ \hline \mathbf{100.24} \end{array}$$

22.
$$\begin{array}{r} 2\overset{3}{1}.\overset{3}{5}5 \\ \times6 \\ \hline \mathbf{129.30} \end{array}$$

23.
$$\begin{array}{r} 2.6 \\ 3\overline{\smash{)}7.8} \\ 6 \\ \hline 1\,8 \\ 1\,8 \\ \hline 0 \end{array}$$

24.
$$\begin{array}{r} 1.05 \\ 5\overline{\smash{)}5.25} \\ 5 \\ \hline 2 \\ 0 \\ \hline 25 \\ 25 \\ \hline 0 \end{array}$$

25.
$$\begin{array}{r} 2.445 \\ 2\overline{\smash{)}4.890} \\ 4 \\ \hline 8 \\ 8 \\ \hline 9 \\ 8 \\ \hline 10 \\ 10 \\ \hline 0 \end{array}$$

26.
$$\begin{array}{r} 4.1 \\ 4\overline{\smash{)}16.4} \\ 16.4 \\ 4 \\ \hline 4 \\ \hline 0 \end{array}$$

27.
$$\begin{array}{r} 3.05 \\ 9\overline{\smash{)}27.45} \\ 27 \\ \hline 4 \\ 0 \\ \hline 45 \\ 45 \\ \hline 0 \end{array}$$

28.
$$\begin{array}{r} 10.85 \\ 4\overline{\smash{)}43.40} \\ 4 \\ \hline 3 \\ 0 \\ \hline 3\,4 \\ 3\,2 \\ \hline 20 \\ 20 \\ \hline 0 \end{array}$$

29.
$$\begin{array}{r} 90.3 \\ 9\overline{\smash{)}812.7} \\ 81 \\ \hline 2 \\ 0 \\ \hline 2\,7 \\ 2\,7 \\ \hline 0 \end{array}$$

30.

```
      67.025
   6)402.15
     36
     ──
      42
      42
     ──
       1
       0
       ─
       15
       12
       ──
        30
        30
        ──
         0
```

31.

```
      3.6
   3)18
     15
     ──
      30
      30
      ──
       0
```

32.

```
      1.25
   8)10.00
     8
     ──
      20
      16
      ──
       40
       40
       ──
        0
```

33. (A) $26.54 + 92.88 \approx 27 + 93 =$ **120**

(C) $84.05 - 77.13 \approx 84 - 77 =$ **7**

(D) $5.4 \times 8 \approx 5 \times 8 =$ **40**

(E) $11.99 \div 3 \approx 12 \div 3 =$ **4**

(I) $125.09 + 68.01 \approx 125 + 68 =$ **193**

(L) $524.87 - 128.39 \approx 525 - 128 =$ **397**

(M) $44.19 \times 5 \approx 44 \times 5 =$ **220**

(S) $35.59 \div 6 \approx 36 \div 6 =$ **6**

DECIMALS

34. Mrs. Abdul 2.4 lb. Mrs. Davidson 1.35 lb. ?

$2.4 + 1.35 = 3.75$ lb.

$2.4 + 3.75 = 6.15$ lb.

They bought **6.15 lb.** of meat altogether.

```
   2.40
 + 1.35
 ──────
   3.75

    1
   2.40
 + 3.75
 ──────
   6.15
```

35. $108.25 | $43.05 | $12.20 | ?

$43.05 + 12.20 = 55.25$

$108.25 - 55.25 = 53$

She had **$53** left.

```
   43.05
 + 12.20
 ──────
   55.25

    0 10
   1̸0̸8.25
 −  55.25
 ──────
   53.00
```

36. 6 kg | R | S | S   4.5 kg   ?

R: Rice
S: Sugar

$6 - 4.5 = 1.5$ kg

Each bag of sugar has a mass of 1.5 kg.

$5 \times 1.5 = 7.5$ kg

The mass of five bags of sugar is **7.5 kg.**

```
    5 10
   6̸.0̸
 − 4.5
 ─────
   1.5

     2
   1.5
 ×   5
 ─────
   7.5
```

37. Tuesday 180.63 mi. | 2.1 mi.   Wednesday ?   1.2 mi.

$180.63 + 2.1 = 182.73$ mi.

$182.73 - 1.2 = 181.53$ mi.

The distance the train traveled on Wednesday was **181.53 mi.**

```
   180.63
 +   2.1
 ──────
   182.73

   182.73
 −   1.2
 ──────
   181.53
```

38. Lily 24.3 kg   Father   ?

$4 \times 24.3 = 97.2$ kg

The total mass of Lily and her father is **97.2 kg.**

```
    1 1
   24.3
 ×    4
 ─────
   97.2
```

39. 21.75 yd. | ? | ? | ?   2.4 yd.

$21.75 - 2.4 = 19.35$ yd.

$19.35 \div 3 = 6.45$ yd.

The length of each of the three pieces of ribbon is **6.45 yd.**

```
    1 11
   2̸1̸.75
 −   2.4
 ──────
   19.35

      6.45
   3)19.35
     18
     ──
      1 3
      1 2
      ───
       15
       15
       ──
        0
```

40. $50 | $11.45 | $11.45 | $11.45 | ?

$3 \times 11.45 = 34.35$

$50 - 34.35 = 15.65$

He would receive **$15.65** in change.

```
    1 1
   11.45
 ×    3
 ─────
   34.35

    4 9 9 10
   5̸0̸.0̸0̸
 − 34.35
 ──────
   15.65
```

41. (a) ? 12.76 gal. | 12.76 gal. | 12.76 gal.

$3 \times 12.76 = 38.28$ gal.

He would need **38.28 gal.** of paint if he wanted to paint three similar rooms.

```
    2 1
   12.76
 ×    3
 ─────
   38.28
```

(b) $38.28 \times 5 = 191.40$

Mr. Mendoza paid **$191.40** for the paint.

```
    4 1 4
   38.28
 ×    5
 ──────
   191.40
```

42. ? 38.25 kg | 0.75 kg | 0.75 kg | 0.75 kg | 0.75 kg | 0.75 kg | 0.75 kg

$6 \times 0.75 = 4.5$ kg

$38.25 + 4.5 = 42.75$ kg

Mr. Woods had **42.75 kg** of sugar in the beginning.

```
    4 3
   0.75
 ×    6
 ─────
   4.50

    1
   38.25
 +  4.5
 ──────
   42.75
```

43. orange juice   apple juice ? $0.35 $6.55

$6.55 + 0.35 = 6.90$

$6.90 \div 3 = 2.30$

The cost of the bottle of orange juice was **$2.30.**

```
    1
   6.55
 + 0.35
 ─────
   6.90

      2.30
   3)6.90
     6
     ──
      9
      9
      ──
      0
      0
      ──
      0
```

Review 5

1. **(3)**
The digit 8 is in the hundredths place.

2. **(2)**
$\dfrac{2^{\times 2}}{5^{\times 2}} = \dfrac{4}{10} = 0.4$

3. **(3)**

5.98 + 1.93 = 7.91

4. **(3)**

$62.458 = 62\frac{458}{1,000} = 62$ ones 458 thousandths

= 62,458 thousandths

5. **(3)**

$37.46 \approx 37.5$

6. **(2)**

$$
\begin{array}{r}
32.07 \\
9\overline{)288.63} \\
\underline{27} \\
18 \\
\underline{18} \\
6 \\
\underline{0} \\
63 \\
\underline{63} \\
0
\end{array}
$$

7. **(3)**

$12.99 + 5.5 \approx 13 + 6 = 19$

8. **540.701**

9. $1.68 = 1 + \frac{68}{100} = 1\frac{68}{100} = 1\frac{17}{25}$

10. **0.4**

11. **0.35**

$9\frac{35}{100} = 9 + 0.35$

12. **5.2 gallons of water**

1.9 + 2.1 + 1.2 = 5.2 gal.

13. **15.4**

1.92 × 8 = 15.36

15.36 ≈ 15.4

14. **19**

305.419 = 3 hundreds 5 ones 4 tenths 1 hundredth
9 thousandths

1 hundredth 9 thousandths = 19 thousandths

15. **5.6, 5.06, 5.006, 0.56**

16. **2.52 m**

```
                3.78 m
Katrina  |‾‾‾‾|‾‾‾‾|‾‾‾‾|
Sarah    |____|
                    ?
```

3.78 ÷ 3 = 1.26 m

2 × 1.26 = 2.52 m

17. **0.69 lb.**

```
          2.76 lb.
| ? | ? | ? | ? |
```

2.76 ÷ 4 = 0.69 lb.

18.

```
              ?
| 12.9 mi. | 12.9 mi. |
```

2 × 12.9 = 25.8 mi.

She travels a total of 25.8 mi. every day.

```
                    ?
| 25.8 mi. | 25.8 mi. | 25.8 mi. | 25.8 mi. | 25.8 mi. |
```

5 × 25.8 = 129 mi.

The total distance traveled by Elsie from Monday to Friday is **129 mi.**

19.

```
                      $2,954.10
| 12 dresses | ? | ? | ? | ? | ? | ? | ? |
  $2,376.60
```

$2,954.10 – $2,376.60 = $577.50

$577.50 ÷ 7 = $82.50

Each blouse cost **$82.50**.

20.

```
             10 m
| 2 blouses | ? | ? | ? | ? |
  3.6 m
```

10 – 3.6 = 6.4 m

6.4 ÷ 4 = 1.6 m

Sheila used **1.6 m** of cloth to sew each skirt.

Unit 11: Time

1. **30**

When the second hand moves from 12 to 6, it is 30 sec.

2. **40**

When the second hand moves from 3 to 11, it is 40 sec.

3. **35**

When the second hand moves from 12 to 7, it is 35 sec.

4. **15**

When the second hand moves from 9 to 12, it is 15 sec.

5. **30**

When the second hand moves from 5 to 11, it is 30 sec.

6.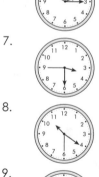

7.

8.

9.

10.

11. **6:38:06 P.M.**

12. **1:22:21 P.M.**

13. **4:40:33 A.M.**

14. **2:30:56 P.M.**

15. **1:02:18 P.M.**

16. **4:44:24 A.M.**

Singapore Math Level 4A & 4B

17. **11:06:05 A.M.**
18. **9:08:13 P.M.**
19. **4:51:05 P.M.**
20. **10:29:02 P.M.**
21. **30 min.**

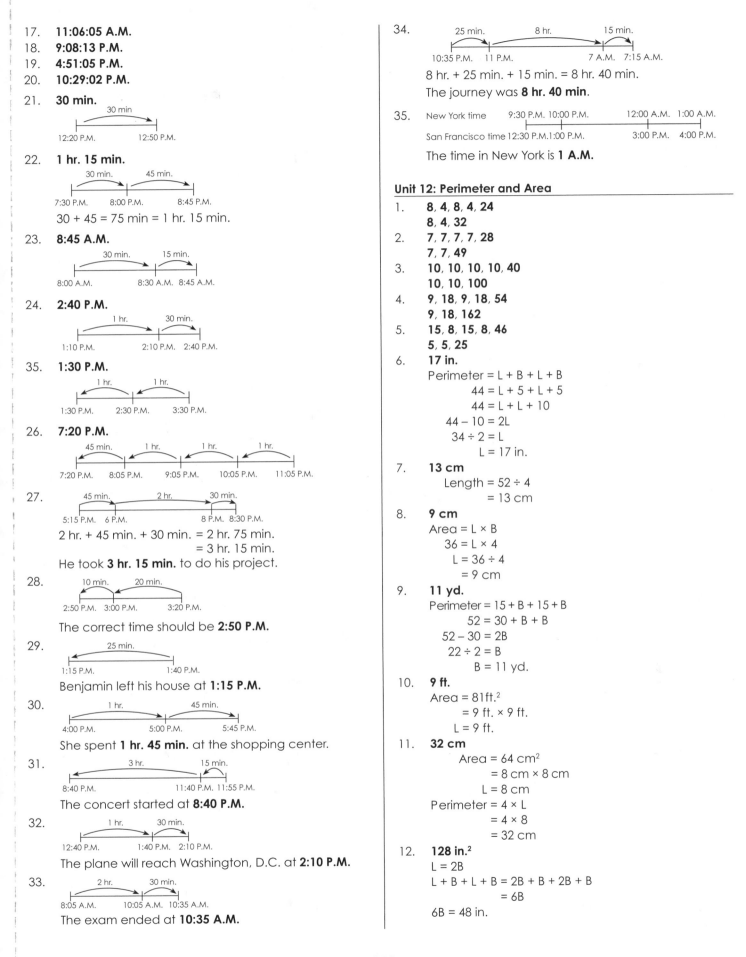

30 min
12:20 P.M.   12:50 P.M.

22. **1 hr. 15 min.**

30 min.   45 min.
7:30 P.M.   8:00 P.M.   8:45 P.M.

30 + 45 = 75 min = 1 hr. 15 min.

23. **8:45 A.M.**

30 min.   15 min.
8:00 A.M.   8:30 A.M. 8:45 A.M.

24. **2:40 P.M.**

1 hr.   30 min.
1:10 P.M.   2:10 P.M. 2:40 P.M.

35. **1:30 P.M.**

1 hr.   1 hr.
1:30 P.M.   2:30 P.M.   3:30 P.M.

26. **7:20 P.M.**

45 min.   1 hr.   1 hr.   1 hr.
7:20 P.M. 8:05 P.M. 9:05 P.M. 10:05 P.M. 11:05 P.M.

27.

45 min.   2 hr.   30 min.
5:15 P.M. 6 P.M.   8 P.M. 8:30 P.M.

2 hr. + 45 min. + 30 min. = 2 hr. 75 min.
= 3 hr. 15 min.

He took **3 hr. 15 min.** to do his project.

28.

10 min.   20 min.
2:50 P.M. 3:00 P.M.   3:20 P.M.

The correct time should be **2:50 P.M.**

29.

25 min.
1:15 P.M.   1:40 P.M.

Benjamin left his house at **1:15 P.M.**

30.

1 hr.   45 min.
4:00 P.M.   5:00 P.M.   5:45 P.M.

She spent **1 hr. 45 min.** at the shopping center.

31.

3 hr.   15 min.
8:40 P.M.   11:40 P.M. 11:55 P.M.

The concert started at **8:40 P.M.**

32.

1 hr.   30 min.
12:40 P.M.   1:40 P.M. 2:10 P.M.

The plane will reach Washington, D.C. at **2:10 P.M.**

33.

2 hr.   30 min.
8:05 A.M.   10:05 A.M. 10:35 A.M.

The exam ended at **10:35 A.M.**

34.

25 min.   8 hr.   15 min.
10:35 P.M. 11 P.M.   7 A.M. 7:15 A.M.

8 hr. + 25 min. + 15 min. = 8 hr. 40 min.
The journey was **8 hr. 40 min.**

35.
New York time   9:30 P.M. 10:00 P.M.   12:00 A.M. 1:00 A.M.

San Francisco time 12:30 P.M.1:00 P.M.   3:00 P.M.   4:00 P.M.

The time in New York is **1 A.M.**

Unit 12: Perimeter and Area

1. **8, 4, 8, 4, 24**
   8, 4, 32
2. **7, 7, 7, 7, 28**
   7, 7, 49
3. **10, 10, 10, 10, 40**
   10, 10, 100
4. **9, 18, 9, 18, 54**
   9, 18, 162
5. **15, 8, 15, 8, 46**
   5, 5, 25
6. **17 in.**
   Perimeter = L + B + L + B
   44 = L + 5 + L + 5
   44 = L + L + 10
   44 − 10 = 2L
   34 ÷ 2 = L
   L = 17 in.
7. **13 cm**
   Length = 52 ÷ 4
   = 13 cm
8. **9 cm**
   Area = L × B
   36 = L × 4
   L = 36 ÷ 4
   = 9 cm
9. **11 yd.**
   Perimeter = 15 + B + 15 + B
   52 = 30 + B + B
   52 − 30 = 2B
   22 ÷ 2 = B
   B = 11 yd.
10. **9 ft.**
    Area = 81ft.²
    = 9 ft. × 9 ft.
    L = 9 ft.
11. **32 cm**
    Area = 64 cm²
    = 8 cm × 8 cm
    L = 8 cm
    Perimeter = 4 × L
    = 4 × 8
    = 32 cm
12. **128 in.²**
    L = 2B
    L + B + L + B = 2B + B + 2B + B
    = 6B
    6B = 48 in.

Singapore Math Level 4A & 4B

B = 48 ÷ 6 = 8 in.
L = 2 × B = 16 in.
Area = 8 × 16 = 128 in.²

13. **2 ft.²**
Perimeter = L + L + B + B
6 = L + L + 1 + 1
L + L = 6 − 2 = 4 ft.
L = 4 ÷ 2 = 2 ft.
Area = 2 × 1 = 2 ft.²

14. **16 m**
Area = L × L
16 m² = 4 m × 4 m
L = 4 m
Perimeter = 4 × 4 = 16 m

15. **50 yd.**
A = L × B
$150 = \frac{3}{2}B \times B$
$150 \div \frac{3}{2} = B \times B$
$150 \times \frac{2}{3} = B \times B$
100 = B × B
B = 10 yd.
$L = \frac{3}{2} \times 10 = 15$ yd.
Perimeter = 10 + 15 + 10 + 15
= 50 yd.

16. **46 cm**

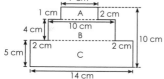

Perimeter
= 9 + 4 + 6 + 4 + 6 + 9 + 8
= 46 cm

17. **84 in.²**

Area of A = 16 × 3 = 48 in.²

Area of B = 9 × 3 = 27 in.²

Area of C = 3 × 3 = 9 in.²

Total area = 48 + 27 + 9 = 84 in.²

18.

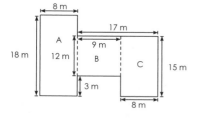

Area of A = 7 × 1 = 7 cm²
Area of B = 10 × 4 = 40 cm²
Area of C = 14 × 5 = 70 cm²
Total area = 7 + 40 + 70 = **117 cm²**
Perimeter = 7 + 1 + 1 + 4 + 2 + 5 + 14 + 10 = **44 cm**

19.

Area of A = 18 × 8 = 144 m²
Area of B = 9 × 12 = 108 m²
Area of C = 15 × 8 = 120 m²
Total area = 144 + 108 + 120 = **372 m²**
Perimeter = 8 + 3 + 17 + 15 + 8 + 3 + 9 + 3 + 8 + 18
= **92 m**

20.

Area of A = 10 × 12 = 120 ft.²
Area of B = 26 × 12 = 312 ft.²
Area of C = 20 × 6 = 120 ft.²
Total area = 120 + 312 + 120 = **552 ft.²**.
Perimeter
= 26 + 12 + 9 + 6 + 20 + 6 + 15 + 6 + 12 + 10 + 12 + 8
= **142 ft.**

21.

Area of A = 15 × 12 = 180 m²

Area of B = 7 × 5 = 35 m²

180 + 35 = 215 m²

Her house is **215 m²**.

22. Area of exhibition hall = 16 × 15 = 240 ft.².
Area that is not covered with carpet
= 9 × 8
= 72 ft.²
240 − 72 = 168 ft.²
The area that is covered with carpet is **168 ft.²**.

23. Area of one square = 294 ÷ 6 = 49 cm² = 7 × 7
Length of each square = 7 cm
12 × 7 = 84 cm
The perimeter of the shaded portion is **84 cm**.

24. Area of the larger rectangular board
= L × B
= (28 + 3 + 3) × (16 + 3 + 3)
= 34 × 22
= 748 in.²
Area of the white rectangular board = L × B
= 28 × 16
= 448 in.²
748 − 448 = 300 in.²
The area not covered by the white rectangular board
is **300 in.²**.

25. Area of Mary's room = L × B
= 8 × 7
= 56 m²
Area not covered by the carpet = L × B
= 4.5 × 4
= 18 m²
56 − 18 = 38 m²
The floor area in her room that is covered by carpet is
38 m².

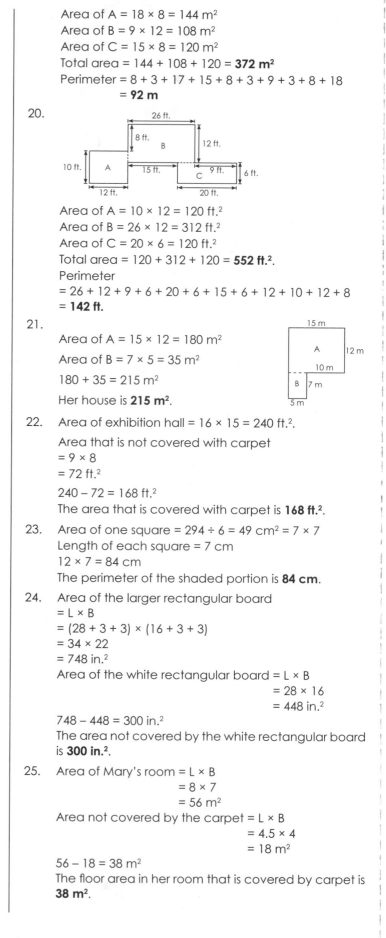

Singapore Math Level 4A & 4B

26. (a) $(15 + 2 + 2) + (11 + 2 + 2) = 34$ yd.
   $2 \times 34 = 68$ yd.
   The length of the fence was **68 yd.**
   (b) $68 \times \$3.85 = \$261.80$
   It cost **\$261.80** to put a fence round the plot of land.

27. Area of the square cardboard = L × L
   $\qquad\qquad\qquad\qquad\qquad = 35 \times 35$
   $\qquad\qquad\qquad\qquad\qquad = 1{,}225 \text{ cm}^2$
   Area of the "L" shape = $(19 \times 5) + (25 \times 6)$
   $\qquad\qquad\qquad\qquad = 245 \text{ cm}^2$
   $1{,}225 - 245 = 980 \text{ cm}^2$
   The remaining area of the cardboard was **980 cm²**.

Review 6

1. **(2)**
   Width = $32 \div 2 = 16$ in.
   Perimeter = $32 + 16 + 32 + 16 = 96$ in.

2. **(2)**

3. **(4)**
   Perimeter = $4 \times 256 = 1{,}024$ m
   $6 \times 1{,}024 = 6{,}144$ m

4. **(2)**
   When the second hand moves from 2 to 6, it is 20 sec.

5. **(3)**
   $6 + 6 + 3 + 3 + 3 + 6 + 6 + 15 = 48$ ft.

6. **(1)**
   $64 - 19 - 19 = 26$ cm
   $26 \div 2 = 13$ cm

7. **(2)**
   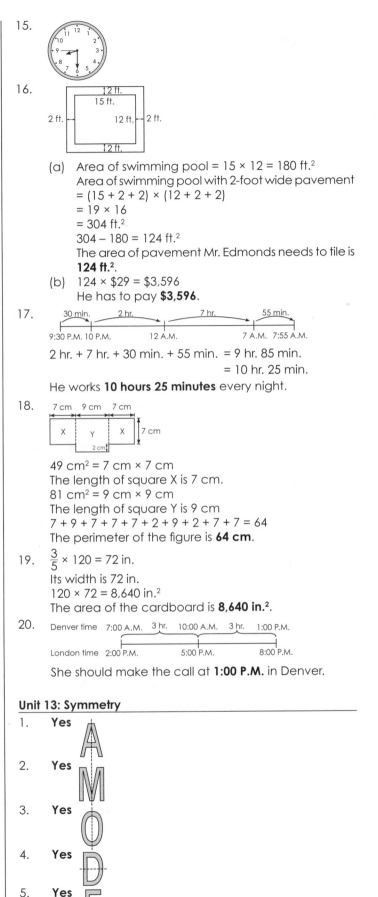
   1 hr. $+ 20$ min. $+ 15$ min. $= 1$ hr. 35 min.

8. Length = $40 \div 4 = 10$ yd.
   Area = $10 \times 10 =$ **100 yd.²**

9. **540 cm²**
   Area A = $8 \times 11 = 88 \text{ cm}^2$
   Area B = $16 \times 11 = 176 \text{ cm}^2$
   Area C = $30 \times 8 = 240 \text{ cm}^2$
   $88 + 176 + 240 = 504 \text{ cm}^2$

10. **8 ft.**
   Area of each square = $256 \div 4 = 64 \text{ ft.}^2 = 8 \times 8$
   Length of each square = 8 ft.

11. **84 in.**
   Area of A = $12 \times 12 = 144 \text{ in.}^2$
   $\qquad\quad 144 = L \times 8$
   $\qquad\qquad L = 144 \div 8 = 18$ in.
   Perimeter = $12 + 12 + 4 + 18 + 8 + 18 + 12 = 84$ in.

12. **112 m²**
   Area of bigger rectangle = $20 \times 14 = 280 \text{ m}^2$
   Area of smaller rectangle = $14 \times 12 = 168 \text{ m}^2$
   Area of shaded part = $280 - 168 = 112 \text{ m}^2$

13. **1:15 P.M.**

14. **10:22:43 P.M.**

15.

16.
   (a) Area of swimming pool = $15 \times 12 = 180 \text{ ft.}^2$
   Area of swimming pool with 2-foot wide pavement
   $= (15 + 2 + 2) \times (12 + 2 + 2)$
   $= 19 \times 16$
   $= 304 \text{ ft.}^2$
   $304 - 180 = 124 \text{ ft.}^2$
   The area of pavement Mr. Edmonds needs to tile is **124 ft.²**.
   (b) $124 \times \$29 = \$3{,}596$
   He has to pay **\$3,596**.

17.
   2 hr. $+ 7$ hr. $+ 30$ min. $+ 55$ min. $= 9$ hr. 85 min.
   $\qquad\qquad\qquad\qquad\qquad\qquad\quad = 10$ hr. 25 min.
   He works **10 hours 25 minutes** every night.

18.
   $49 \text{ cm}^2 = 7 \text{ cm} \times 7 \text{ cm}$
   The length of square X is 7 cm.
   $81 \text{ cm}^2 = 9 \text{ cm} \times 9 \text{ cm}$
   The length of square Y is 9 cm
   $7 + 9 + 7 + 7 + 7 + 2 + 9 + 2 + 7 + 7 = 64$
   The perimeter of the figure is **64 cm**.

19. $\dfrac{3}{5} \times 120 = 72$ in.
   Its width is 72 in.
   $120 \times 72 = 8{,}640 \text{ in.}^2$
   The area of the cardboard is **8,640 in.²**.

20.
   She should make the call at **1:00 P.M.** in Denver.

Unit 13: Symmetry

1. **Yes**

2. **Yes**

3. **Yes**

4. **Yes**

5. **Yes**

Singapore Math Level 4A & 4B

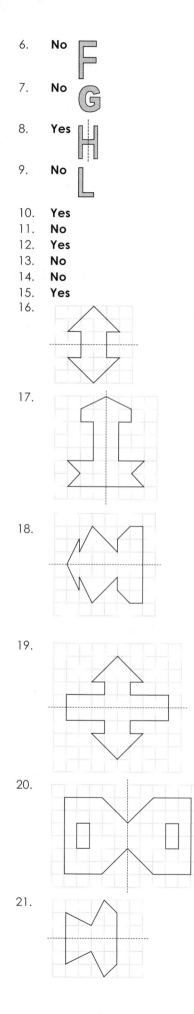

6. **No**
7. **No**
8. **Yes**
9. **No**
10. **Yes**
11. **No**
12. **Yes**
13. **No**
14. **No**
15. **Yes**
16.
17.
18.
19.
20.
21.

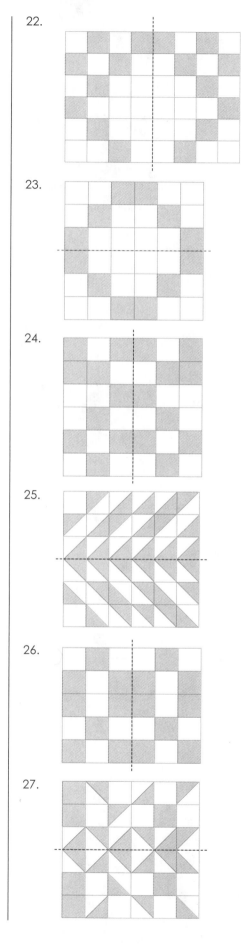

22.
23.
24.
25.
26.
27.

Singapore Math Level 4A & 4B

Unit 14: Tessellations

For questions 1 to 5, accept other correct answers.

1.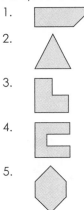

2.

3.

4.

5.

6. **No**
The gaps show that the shape does not tessellate.

7. **Yes**

8. **No**
The gaps show that the shape does not tessellate.

9. **Yes**

10. **Yes**

11.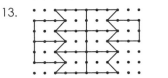

12.

13.

14.

15.

16. (a)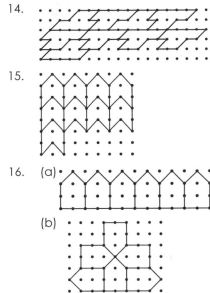

    (b)

17. (a)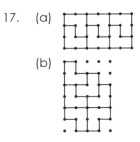

    (b)

Review 7

1. **(2)**
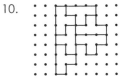

2. **(2)**

3. **(3)**
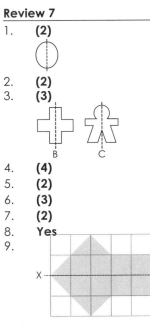

4. **(4)**

5. **(2)**

6. **(3)**

7. **(2)**

8. **Yes**

9.
X ———————— Y

10.

11. *Accept other correct answers.*

12. **Yes**

13.

14.

15.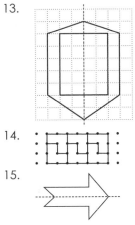

247

Singapore Math Level 4A & 4B

16. **No**

17. *Accept other correct answers.*

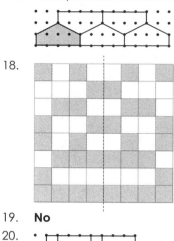

18.

19. **No**

20.

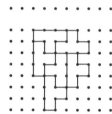

Final Review

1. **(3)**
   $28.16 + 5.09 = 33.25$

2. **(2)**
   $4 \text{ m } 60 \text{ cm} \approx 5 \text{ m}$

3. **(3)**
   When the second hand moves from 3 to 8, it is 25 sec.

4. **(1)**

5. **(4)**
   $8.604 = 8 + 0.6 + 0.004$

6. **(2)**

7. **(4)**
   $40 + 1.5 + 0.03 = 41.53$

8. **(3)**

9. **(1)**
   $64 \div 4 = 16 \text{ in.}$

10. **(2)**
    $405 \text{ hundredths} = \frac{405}{100} = 4\frac{5}{100} = 4.05$

11. **(4)**
    $93.28 \times 8 = 746.24$

12. **(3)**

13. **(2)**

    30 min.   1 hr.   10 min.

    7:30 P.M. 8:00 P.M.   9:00 P.M. 9:10 P.M.

    1 hr. + 30 min. + 10 min. = 1 hr. 40 min.

14. **(2)**

$5.4 \div 4 = 1.35$

15. **(1)**
    $100 \div 10 = 10$
    $10 \times \$2.05 = \$20.50$

16. **(1)**
    $18.35 - 3.2 = 15.15 \text{ sec.}$

17. **(2)**
    Length $= 20 \div 4 = 5 \text{ ft.}$
    Area $= 5 \times 5 = 25 \text{ ft.}^2$

18. **(3)**
    Perimeter $= 12 \times 4 = 48 \text{ cm}$

19. **(2)**
    $9.9 \approx 10$

20. **(4)**
    The digit 9 is in the thousandths place.

21. **0.5**
    $\frac{8}{16} = \frac{1^{\times 5}}{2_{\times 5}} = \frac{5}{10} = 0.5$

22. **1:10 P.M.**

    1 hr. 1 hr. 1 hr. 45 min. 10 min.

    9:15 A.M. 10:15 A.M. 11:15 A.M. 12:15 P.M. 1:00 P.M. 1:10 P.M.

23. **0.8**
    $\frac{4^{\times 2}}{5_{\times 2}} = \frac{8}{10} = 0.8$

24. **Shade any 3 squares.**
    $\frac{25}{100} \times 12 = 3$

25. **Yes**

26. *Accept other correct answers.*

27. **7.8, 7.08, 0.78**

28. **255 m²**

    Area of A $= 12 \times 5 = 60 \text{ m}^2$
    Area of B $= 12 \times 5 = 60 \text{ m}^2$
    Area of C $= 27 \times 5 = 135 \text{ m}^2$
    Total area $= 60 + 60 + 135 = 255 \text{ m}^2$

Singapore Math Level 4A & 4B

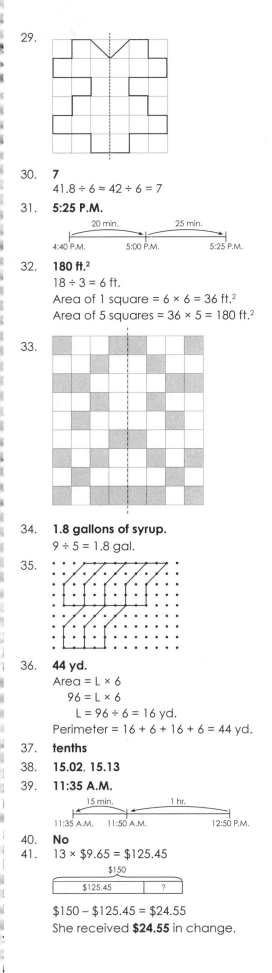

29.

30. **7**
$41.8 ÷ 6 ≈ 42 ÷ 6 = 7$

31. **5:25 P.M.**

20 min.   25 min.
4:40 P.M.   5:00 P.M.   5:25 P.M.

32. **180 ft.²**
$18 ÷ 3 = 6$ ft.
Area of 1 square $= 6 × 6 = 36$ ft.²
Area of 5 squares $= 36 × 5 = 180$ ft.²

33.

34. **1.8 gallons of syrup.**
$9 ÷ 5 = 1.8$ gal.

35.

36. **44 yd.**
Area $= L × 6$
$96 = L × 6$
$L = 96 ÷ 6 = 16$ yd.
Perimeter $= 16 + 6 + 16 + 6 = 44$ yd.

37. **tenths**

38. **15.02**, **15.13**

39. **11:35 A.M.**

15 min.   1 hr.
11:35 A.M.   11:50 A.M.   12:50 P.M.

40. **No**

41. $13 × \$9.65 = \$125.45$

$150
$125.45   ?

$\$150 - \$125.45 = \$24.55$
She received **$24.55** in change.

42.

1 hr.   1 hr.   1 hr.   40 min.
7:05 P.M. 8:05 P.M. 9:05 P.M. 10:05 P.M. 10:45 P.M.

The coach stopped for a rest at 10:45 P.M.

10 min. 1 hr.   1 hr.   1 hr.   1 hr.
11:20 P.M. 11:30 P.M. 0:30 A.M. 1:30 A.M. 2:30 A.M. 3:30 A.M.

The coach continued the journey at 11:20 P.M.

15 min.   20 min.
10:45 P.M.   11:00 P.M.   11:20 P.M.

$15 + 20 = 35$ min.
It stopped **35 min.** for a rest.

43.

?
0.84 L 0.47 L 0.65 L

$0.84 + 0.47 + 0.65 = 1.96$ L
$12 × 1.96 = 23.52$ L
There are **23.52 L** of fruit punch in a dozen bottles.

44.

5 m
1.6 m 95 cm ?

$0.95 + 1.6 = 2.55$ m   [95 cm $= 0.95$ m]
$5 - 2.55 = 2.45$ m
She had **2.45 m** of ribbon left.

45. $18 - 3 - 3 = 12$ yd.
$12 × 12 = 144$ yd.
$144 × \$19 = \$2,736$
The total cost of the carpet is **$2,736**.

Challenge Questions

1.

2. **3 P.M.**

3. $2 × \$919.70 = \$1,839.40$
Four television sets and two DVD players cost $1,839.40.
$\$1,839.40 - \$639.70 = \$1,199.70$
Three television sets cost **$1,199.70.**

4. Area of bigger square $= 576$ in.² $= 24 × 24$
Length of bigger square $= 24$ in.
Area of shaded square $= 144$ in.² $= 12 × 12$
Length of shaded square $= 12$ in.
$2x = 24 - 12 = 12$ in.
$x = 12 ÷ 2 =$ **6 in.**

Singapore Math Level 4A & 4B

5. Perimeter = (8 × 3) + (6 × 3) + (6 × 3) + (4 × 3)
   = **72 cm**

6.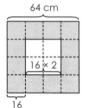

   2 L 600 mL ÷ 2 = 1 L 300 mL

   8 × 1 L 300 mL = 10 L 400 mL

   Mrs. Munoz sold **10 L 400 mL** of lemon tea over the weekend.

7. $3 × 3 × 3 = 27 \text{ in.}^3$
   27 cubes are needed to make this 3-in. solid.

8.

   B: Book
   D: Dictionary

   $85.50 − $37.80 = $47.70

   Two books and a dictionary cost $47.70.

   $47.70 − $37.80 = $9.90

   Each book is **$9.90**.

9.

   64 ÷ 4 = 16 cm
   16 × 2 = 32 cm
   Area of the unshaded square = 32 × 32 = **1,024 cm²**

10.

11. $5 × 5 × 5 = 125 \text{ cm}^3$
    3,125 ÷ 125 = 25
    25 5-cm cubes are needed to form a solid of 3,125 cm³.

12. 1 hour → 5 chairs
    8 hours → 5 × 8 = 40 chairs
    120 ÷ 40 = 3
    He took **3 days** to paint 120 similar chairs.

Singapore Math Level 4A & 4B

Notes

Singapore Math Level 4A & 4B

Notes

Singapore Math Level 4A & 4B

Notes

Notes

Notes

Notes